CW00421930

© 2020 Ramesh Subramaniam

ISBN: 9798714719653

Imprint: Independently published

Ramesh Subramaniam

Practical Learnings from Great Managers

Ramesh Subramaniam

PRACTICAL LESSONS FROM GREAT MANAGERS

FOREWORD

It was at the age of twenty-one that I started my career. Over the past fifty years, I have worked in some of the best companies in India. I had opportunities to work in manufacturing as well as marketing. The last fifty years have been significant for the Indian industry, with shifts in landscape driven by technological advances and easier access to the global marketplace, coupled with continuously evolving customer preferences. Our economy has moved from one of strict controls to a liberalized one. This has increased competition and brought fresh challenges for the Indian companies.

My journey as a manager has been one of continuous learning and adaptation. With new roles and transitions came new challenges and an opportunity to learn from both the people around me and the situations that presented themselves. Books on management, particularly those applicable to the Indian context, were few. Learnings came primarily on the job and through mentors and word of mouth.

This book is my attempt to capture some of the learnings from people I have admired through the course of my career and whose wisdom I have applied and carried forward both professionally and personally. These are practical learnings that teach you to think on your feet and adapt to different situations, learnings you rarely find in management books or management schools. I hope this book will be useful for young managers. It has been written with a view to encouraging them to understand and value practical knowledge and use it appropriately.

My wife and sons are responsible for collecting my notes, which were in chronological order, reordering, editing, and ensuring that the material was encompassed between the two covers of a book. I would like to thank Mrs. Lakshmi Venkatsubramanian for proof reading this book. I also received several suggestions from my family members and close friends. I am grateful to all of them.

Practical Lessons From Great Managers

RAMESH SUBRAMANIAM

Chapters

CHAPTER ONE

Out on my own

It was in April 1971 that I started looking for a job. I was due to complete a Masters degree at IIT Mumbai in May. After graduation, most of us had two options - pursue science and study further, or work in the manufacturing or services sector. Dr. S. H. Patil, one of my professors, gave some excellent advice: "If you pursue Science, you will gain recognition and a big following provided you are in the top ten percent. You will not make much money. On the other hand, in industry, you can make money but perhaps not have the same reputation as a scientist".

Some of my classmates planned to go abroad for further studies, an option that was not available to most, given the lack of financial resources. At the back of our minds, each of us knew that we could always fall back on IIT and enrol in a PhD programme. There would be a monthly stipend of Rs. 250, ensuring a comfortable life for one person. With it came additional advantages of accommodation, lower work pressure, and access to a vast library. Some used this time to contemplate future career options or prepare for entrance examinations. One of my batch mates, Sheel Kant Sharma, not only completed his Ph.D. in about three years but also got into the Foreign Service, rising up the ranks and finally retiring as Secretary-General of SAARC.

Mumbai had several top manufacturing and trading companies that were recruiting, and finding employment at that time was not particularly difficult. The IT industry was in its infancy, offering jobs easily but at meager salaries. Tata Consultancy Service, for example, paid only Rs. 350 per month as the starting salary for college recruits. While these salaries were low, it is worth noting that many of the top executives at TCS today grew from these humble beginnings.

My batch mates and I were mostly from middle class families. In retrospect, even while we needed to be economically independent, we did not have materialistic goals or crave for luxuries that money could offer. Our needs were simple; IIT had given us the breadth, but not the depth of knowledge, and we were still untested in the real world. Our main goal was to get practical experience in a good organization and build a strong foundation.

Today, job applicants often go for a higher salary instead of thinking long term and chasing job content. Even in those days, there were people who got jobs where remuneration was high, such as jobs in foreign banks, but the tasks were often so mundane that they offered little scope for learning and development.

I had registered with the Placement cell at IIT. On the notice board outside their office was a list of companies with job openings. Two companies caught my fancy, and I sent applications to both. One was

Crompton Greaves in Mumbai, and the other was Bata India Limited in Kolkata. Both companies replied and called me for an interview. I decided to meet the powers that be in Bata India, as the interview was in Delhi and I was entitled to train travel by first class. I could also get to meet my cousins who lived there. I cleared this interview. The final interview was in Kolkata, where my parents lived, and I was happy to get a paid ticket to go home.

The panel for the final interview was headed by Mr. Raman, who had retired from the ICS and was an excellent judge of people. He questioned candidates in a manner that enabled him to gauge the aptitude and attitude of the job aspirant. I was lucky to be selected as a management trainee with a salary of Rs 650 per month in addition to some allowances. The training was for two years in marketing.

The interviews at Bata were exceptionally well organized by the then Management Development Advisor Mr. Prem Seth and his assistant Mr. Rajpal. Mr. Seth had a phenomenal memory. He remembered every trainee by name and could rattle out all details from the resume of the trainee. This was not an ordinary feat considering the fact that there were between 100 to 150 trainees spread over various batches. He was a very charismatic leader and could convince any candidate to take up the job.

Over the next fifty years, I worked with Bata, Tata, UNIDO, and Sri City. I had the good fortune of meeting exceptional people and learning from their value systems. Barring a few potholes along the way that were par for the course, my career path has been reasonably smooth. I have been fortunate to have able mentors to guide me through the potholes. I have learnt much from their unique strategies and out-of-the-box thinking.

The aim of sharing my experiences is to acknowledge the contribution to industry by people from whom I have learnt and whose names I want to keep alive. It is also my intense desire that the younger generation looks at their careers with the right perspective and learns from the experiences of the older generation. A job should not just be a means to an end - salary for sustenance. It should be a means not only for personal growth, but also a way to give back to society and our environment. A career should be shaped by a strong value system and a desire to contribute to a cause beyond one's own. It is only then that one can truly enjoy each day of work. The world is not going to remember you for the money you gained. It will remember you for the wealth of good you left behind. This book is in honor and memory of a few of those people that thought beyond themselves and left behind a wealth of knowledge that has shaped countless individuals, including me, in their careers.

A note for my readers: my first draft had my narration in chronological order. I went back memory lane and put down all my experiences as I went along the time axis. In my next draft, I decided to club together learning experiences that belonged to the same category but from different sources. This threw chronology to the winds. I jumped back and forth, from experiences in one company to experiences in another. I sincerely hope that this does not create any confusion.

Dear Reader, do not ask what your workplace can do for you. Ask what you can do for your workplace. Slowly and surely, a lot of pieces will fall into place. You will enjoy your work and, as a result, be a healthier, happier person.

CHAPTER TWO

Bata days - Training through tasks

The Bata shoe organization is a global company founded by Mr. Thomas Bata, a Czech national. When I joined Bata, it consisted of 93 companies spread across the world. The company had its headquarters in Canada, where Mr. Bata had moved post the communist takeover of Czechoslovakia. The Bata company in India was called Bata India and had 24,000 employees. With over 1,200 stores, close to 14,000 wholesale dealers, and production and sales of over 52 million pairs of shoes each year, Bata India was a market leader in the Indian footwear industry.

To understand the type of organization Bata India was and why it became a market leader, it is important to delve into its history in India. Prior to partition in 1947, Bata India had many Muslim workers, with Hindus generally reluctant to enter the leather trade due to religious beliefs. In the wake of partition, there was an exodus of

Muslims to Bangladesh (erstwhile East Pakistan), and Hindus from Pakistan into India.

With the mass exodus, the company was obliged to cater to then Prime Minister Pandit Jawaharlal Nehru's request to accommodate the new migrants in Calcutta (now Kolkata) and Faridabad. In return, the company was given land by the government and additional incentives that temporarily restricted market access to other players. Carona Sahu was the only main competitor at that time.

The migrant employees were mostly illiterate and this necessitated innovative strategies to increase productivity. In subsequent years, the recruitment of qualified people became increasingly challenging. Personnel managers from Bata would wait outside college gates for hours and look for men in good health to pursuade them to join the company as sales staff or store managers. Willingness to work hard was the primary criteria - their educational record did not matter. These recruiting personnel showed that you could make outstanding personnel out of people who had the right attitude and dedication, but missing the educational credentials. There are countless stories of people who joined Bata India this way and rose up the ranks. People like Amalendu Majumdar (Asst. Sales Manager), B Dey (Sales Manager), A R Gupta (Sales Manager) were examples of ordinary people who rose to be excellent managers, respected by all for their ability. This recruitment strategy wasn't new to Bata. Bata already had on its rolls several Czech nationals who could not boast of high educational qualifications, but had the right instincts and attitude, and were extremely hard working and dedicated to their jobs. They were role models for others in the company. Bata made the most of its resources, overcoming recruiting challenges by pivoting attention to developing the right leaders. The slogan in the company at the time, "It CAN be done", was reflective of how Bata developed its leaders.

In the early seventies, Bata operated its worldwide operations across 93 companies with few managers who had the educational credentials, depending largely on a pool of managers who had very basic education skills but who learnt on the job and grew into managers through Bata's rigorous training. In India too, there were particular challenges hiring qualified candidates given the lack of MBAs, or chartered accountants, or qualified engineers. In 1973, when the company went public, there was a requirement to list the top managers along with their qualifications and salaries. This put the company in a dilemma, given most of the top managers lacked the basic educational qualifications one would think would be necessary for such roles. As a workaround, their educational qualifications were listed simply as "MSLC", with no further explanation provided. My colleague Vikas Toley, on seeing this, went up to his training manager asking for details on how he could get a MSLC degree. The training manager laughed and told him he could never get it because he was over qualified. MSLC stood for "Middle School Leaving Certificate".

Over the years, the company continued to rely heavily on the experience of its managers to run operations across the country. While the crop of ingrown managers were an asset, it soon also became a risk. Many of these managers started approaching retirement age, exposing the company to risks of an inadequate replacement pipeline for these impending exits. Seeing this as a critical gap, Mr. Prem Seth started the management trainee programme in India, with a goal of creating a continuous pipeline of budding managers to take on the helms from people retiring. This was a rigorous two-year programme that introduced participants to all aspects of the organization, setting them up for broader roles in the future. The training was highly structured, with particular focus on standards and evaluation methodology. Training tasks ranged from the menial to the white collared. Every trainee was supplied with a manual, the likes of which I have never seen since, in terms of meticulousness, depth and breadth, which were all exemplary.

The Training Manager at the time was Mr. Reginald, a very knowledgeable but stern taskmaster. He was the equivalent of a drill sergeant in the Army – feared, but also respected. Our batch consisted of twelve trainees. For trainees like me, the emphasis was on marketing. The expectation was for us to work at every level in the marketing organization to build an understanding of how people worked at each level, along with the challenges faced by people at those levels. We were expected to be more proficient than the existing employees in those roles.

The Bata training was rigorous, with clearly defined tasks, goals, and standards of achievement laid out for each trainee. We had one job to learn every month or so, and at the end of four months, we had to take a written test and achieve a minimum of 80%. If we failed in this, our training would be extended by a month.

The two- year training process would make marketing managers out of us. More importantly, there were innumerable lessons of life we learnt. These were lessons that silently got into our systems while we battled with data, sales, orders, profits and losses, inventory, and all the processes in a market economy. It is these lessons that I put forth in the rest of the book.

Many of these lessons were about making the right judgement calls and making bets on people that would pay off in the long term. My time at Bata allowed me to observe many such cases. Mr B S Choudhary was a union leader controlling 12,000 employees in Batanagar near Kolkata. The Managing Director, who was a foreigner, met him at several union meetings and felt that he had good managerial capabilities. One day he called him and asked him to join as the Personnel Manager of the company. Normally union leaders are given jobs at the junior officer level to placate them, but in this case, a union leader was offered the highest post in HR. Mr Choudhary accepted this and lived up to the expectations, earning the reputation of being a very effective manager. This strategy was truly out of the box thinking on the part of the Managing director.

At times, creative approaches need to be applied to be effective, approaches that no management book would teach you. What Mr. Choudhary was really good at was driving change through his excellent understanding of human behavior. At Batanagar, all officers were required to sign attendance in a register kept at the entrance. We were supposed to reach at 9 am. Mr. Choudhary instructed the security officer to remove the register at 9.05 am every day and keep it on a small table in his room. Anybody coming late, would have to go into his room and sign. Mr Choudhary would not say a word but the embarrassment for the employee was acute. Many of us would rather apply for half a day leave and work nonetheless instead of going to his room to sign. Tardiness amongst officers became a thing of the past, and it was remarkable how this was achieved without a spoken word from the personnel manager.

During my training, I was made to sit with Mr. Choudhary for some union meetings. I was not allowed to speak and was asked to observe. The union leaders in Kolkata were extremely sharp, well versed in the legalities, and adept at making forceful pro-union arguments. Mr. Choudhary would brief us on how to handle these union meetings The most important thing was to be very intentional with words, because one wrong word uttered could lead to a situation spiraling out of control and words taken out of context, giving leverage to the other party and leading to a weaker negotiation position, or digressing away from an important issue. He was also a very good listener and would let the union leaders say what they wanted. This helped as a stress buster and helped them release a lot of anger and frustrations. He also taught us to concede small matters and bargain on the important ones. He brought home the necessity for preparing meticulously for such meetings so that the management was not caught on the wrong foot.

Observing and listening carefully are critical qualities that are often undermined in today's world. My son works for a high-end software company based in the US. They have a very tough selection system to ensure they are hiring the best, where very few, even those from top ranking institutions, making the final cut. During the final interview, an expert is flown in from the US. This expert sits through the entire interview without saying a word, only observing. The company recruits a person only if this person approves. What this person is looking for are queues on how the candidate approaches problems, whether the candidate has the right soft skills to be successful, and nuances on attitude and behavior that require keen observation. This process also results in lower attrition rates in the long term, as it help attract people who fit well with the culture of the company. Imagine this expert travelling all the way to India and returning back to USA without saying a word during the interview. This is the power of silence. We need to learn more about such techniques in India.

CHAPTER THREE

Training the mind

On the very first day, Mr Reginald told us that Bata wanted hard working, sincere and healthy managers. In the first year of training, a trainee could avail of only one week of leave. Any extension of the leave might lead to a pink slip. Some saving grace though… death of a parent or one's marriage would entitle one to a few more days of leave.

During my training, I was posted as Manager of a retail store in Secunderabad, in south India. I fell ill with Jaundice and went to an allopathic doctor, who told me that I would need to take complete rest for 21 days. I explained to him that I would lose my job if I took 21 days leave and wanted a quicker cure. He then laughed and directed me to a local physician who was very famous for curing jaundice cases. Most people in India know that allopathy has no cure for jaundice and resort to faith healers and the like. I went to the recommended local physician and he took a sample of my urine and looked at it. He proceeded to take some medicine and inserted the medicine into a ripe banana. He then hung the banana in his house and asked me to come back the next morning. When I went back, I was asked to eat the banana. I was cured in three days and was back to work.

I learnt a very useful lesson as a result of this sickness. If you have the mental strength, you can avoid most sicknesses. In my case, the fear of losing my job, helped me build this strength. In the last 48 years, I have never had any serious illness and it has been likewise with my batch mates too. The Army also builds this capability in their recruits. During the Board examinations in India, teachers of the Twelfth grade have a very tough time. They are responsible for the academic results of these students whose careers depend on the grades they get. I have rarely heard of any Twelfth grade teacher fall sick during the board exam. We need to learn how to build this capability. A distant relative of mine, who lived like a Sanyasi (hermit) in Mumbai, travelled to the Himalayas regularly. Once he lost his wooden clogs and went barefoot over eighteen kilometers on a glacier. Mental strength can do wonders to all of us.

Today, many young managers frequently fall ill, and in many cases this is psychological. They are unable to withstand the pressures of work, or unable to complete tasks on time whereby falling sick is a good excuse. Training the mind to battle such pressures and stay ahead is critical to being successful in the long term, especially in the fast paced environment of today.

Punctuality

The other lesson I learnt was to be punctual. We had to report every day at 9 am at the training centre . A late arrival of more than three days in a month would warrant immediate dismissal, with a months pay handed over at the reception.

Lack of punctuality can be a great source of embarrassment to ones self and a source of much hardship to others.

In early 1980, while working for Tata Exports, I went to UK on a marketing visit and had an appointment with a buyer of a large footwear chain. I reached his office about 20 minutes late and thought nothing of it. The Buyer was furious for my being late and said I should have called him if I was running late. Telephones were not easily accessible in those days. He calmed down a few minutes later and took me to his room. His table was clean and had no papers on it. He said that in anticipation of our meeting he had kept all his other work aside and was only waiting for me. This was a great lesson and after that I have rarely been late for any official meeting. I understood the importance of time after this visit.

Managing Time

During my Bata days, I found that every senior Czech manager who worked in the company had a time table for each day. They listed the activities in order of priority, and allotted time slots for each of the activities. Nothing escaped their attention while they covered each activity systematically. Their work ethic was flawless. In case they were behind schedule, they would come very early to the office and catch up on their work. The daily time-table was neatly typed and kept under the glass of their tabletop.

These managers understood the importance of time management and allotted time according to the importance of each issue. Many managers today are unable to schedule their activities, even when they have secretaries to whom they can delegate the planning.

The other thing I learnt is that while they went into detail they would not go into areas which were monitored by others under them. They worked on a horizontal plane of organization, but learned to delegate work to others and hold them responsible. Every top manager should have a list of things that they should do and things that they should not do, but delegate.

Understanding the context of why a task is needed and its severity is important to determine how much time should be allocated. I have seen many managers spend hours on a trivial issue where the cost benefit was minimal. On the other hand, they would spend minimum time on issues having major implications for the company. As an example, managers routinely go to the accounts department to get the latest updates on sales and turnovers. The accountants however often spend more time than needed trying to be precise, whereas the broader context is often around getting an approximate figure that is reasonably accurate figure to drive decisions, not a figure accurate to the second decimal place!

CHAPTER FOUR

A passion for learning

Sources of knowledge are all around us - books, nature, mentors, trainers, newspapers, and an entire gamut of other resources. It is up to each individual to make maximum use of available resources to grow intellectually and equip oneself to deal with the world. It is important that a person has a positive attitude and the ability to extract the best out of every situation.

People are not good or bad. There is goodness or badness in them. With this in mind, one can learn from the good points in the people we interact with. Similarly, situations can be good or bad. There are lessons to be learnt, even in bad situations. Every experience is a teacher. A tree absorbs water, nutrients from the soil, uses sunlight, and grows. In return, it gives shade, fruits, flowers, and oxygen. There are trees whose every part is useful. So too must a human being absorb all that he or she can, to grow intellectually and be a useful member of the society.

I was at Bata France in 1978 on a training programme, in Hellocourt, near Nancy. We had a swimming instructor who asked us to jump into a pool and swim irrespective of whether or not we knew how to. He had a long pole, which he would thrust towards a distressed swimmer. Needless to say, most of us learnt the art of swimming in a very natural manner. In a do or die situation, you end up performing.

In 1973, I was working as a management trainee at the Bata Stores in Kolkata. During the Durga Puja sales, the busiest time of the year, we ran out of some critical stock that was produced in Patna. Puja in Kolkata is like Christmas in western countries. During Puja time, sales are at a peak. Normally, 30% of the annual sales in Kolkata were achieved in six weeks of Puja sales. A lot of spadework had to be done to meet the demand.

The Assistant Sales Manager, Mr. Majumdar, sent me to Patna by the overnight train and I was to return the next evening with all the merchandise. It was a do or die situation. I reached the factory in Patna at 6.30 am. With the aid of my colleagues there, I gathered the required materials and got it packed in forty seven large wooden cases, which occupied half a truck when loaded. The packing, loading, and invoicing was completed by 4 pm. I reached Patna station and was to catch the train which originated at Delhi and went via Patna to Kolkata. The stop at Patna was only for five minutes, during which time I had to load all the goods.

The railway staff told me that this was totally impossible. It would take at least 2 minutes to open the brake van, and we would have just three minutes for the loading. Our packer, who had come from the factory, gave me an idea. He asked me not to worry about the loading as he would take care of it. I was to go to the engine driver and somehow convince him to stall the train for a few more minutes.

The engine driver was a sombre Anglo Indian. I told him that I would lose my job if I did not load the goods and would not be able to get another job easily. I requested his help, and he smiled and agreed. The goods were loaded, and I boarded the same train. The next morning, I was met at the station by my batchmate, R. S. Agarwal, who helped me clear the goods and reach the office by 9:30 AM. An impossible task was achieved in this challenging situation. The human factor was also responsible - the goodwill of all those who helped me achieve what seemed to be impossible.

During Puja of another year, I was posted at a small store in the Lake market area of Kolkata. The area of the shop was only around 400 square feet. My job was to handle Puja sales and assist the manager, Mr. Das. He was senior in age and told me at the very first meeting that my educational qualifications and the certificates I possessed could never compensate for the years of experience he had and that I would not be able to do the job. He had a very negative attitude and it was obvious he did not want me around. However, he had to follow company directions and was stuck with me for the next six weeks. He ordered me to set up a stall on the footpath outside the store and show my sales skills from there and not from inside the store. I accepted this challenge and spent six weeks selling shoes on the footpath. My parents were very embarrassed to see their son, not only standing on the footpath but also selling shoes. I did well, and on the last day, the manager called me in, appreciated my work, and said that he did not believe I would be able to boost the sales in such a short time. He called all the staff and gave me sweets, and also spoke to my regional manager praising my work.

The method of training was to drop trainees in difficult situations and let them swim against the tide. In the long run, this helped because later, when I worked as a District Manager, I knew the job well and was clear about what areas needed attention and control.

Going back to the swimming pool instructor, when driving me to the pool, he taught me about the rules governing driving in France. It was an eye-opener for me. He told me the art of overtaking a vehicle. He also told me about the importance and safety aspects of having powerful engines, which enabled one to overtake on a sharper curve. In India, people drive without knowing the rules. Overtaking from the left is a common occurrence. This causes so many accidents. Rules need to be made and also strictly adhered to, not only for traffic but also in all walks of life. Rules followed with strict adherence reduce a lot of the complex problems that can arise in a company.

Bata had very elaborate cost accounting and financial accounting systems, and along with them came strict compliance rules. The company had over 500 lines of stock, 1200 stores, 14,000 wholesalers and nearly 24,000 employees. Yet, the company had excellent systems at the store and factory levels to tally all stocks in quantity and value. Shortages in stock or cash at the store level were payable by the store managers. As a District Manager, I was responsible for around 30 stores, all within a 250 km distance from where I was stationed. I was required to take physical inventories in each store at least once in ten weeks. These were surprise checks and were quite laborious since we did not have electronic devices, and all checking was manual. There were stores with about 5,000 pairs of stock, and counting each of these was not easy. At each store, inventories had to be tallied both in-stock quantity and cash, and discrepancies reported. An important rule was that District Managers were responsible for major shortages for six months after their tenure. Major stock shortages do not happen overnight and are often signs of gaps in processes. The company had found that the negligence of the District Manager during the checking process was one of the major contributors to these shortages. To address this, the company instituted a 'six month responsibility' rule. I personally found that it was easy to complete surprise checks within ten weeks in all my stores and tally the stock and cash perfectly.

Over time, such rules have lost the rigorous compliance that is needed to achieve the desired outcomes. Companies have paid the price by having large shortages and a surge in false reporting of inventories, owing to District Managers delegating their responsibilities to other individuals or having misplaced trust in the shop manager. Procedures and rules have to be simple and clear but applied very rigidly with high standards of documentation to prevent fraud and ensure the process works as intended.

There is a lot of wisdom in maintaining a running log of matters of importance, a practice frequently followed by the earlier generations, often in pocket notebooks: births, details of family members, daily expenses, wedding planning, and addresses. Even today, in the age of computers and mobile phones, there are many moments when one realizes the importance of having a pocket notebook.

Whenever Mr. Bata visited India, the company would nominate a trainee to be his aide during the duration of his trip. Trainees in the company were required to maintain records in a small pocket notebook. The nominated trainee would be given three weeks of preparation time to collect statistics related to the company and note down relevant data in a small six punch pocket diary. The trainee would thus have answers handy when needed and would not cut a sorry figure in front of Mr. Bata when asked for information.

This procedure was also required whenever a person travelled overseas. I did this during my first trip overseas, jotting down copious amounts of information about companies and their operations. The procedure was put in place to ensure that employees had the discipline to jot down important information and had the facts readily available when asked.

Many years later, when I worked for Tata International, a particular interaction with a senior executive served as a reminder of the importance of carrying a pen and notebook. This was one time when I was at the office of Lt. Gen Malhotra, the then Director, to get some approvals. In our discussion, Lt. Gen Malhotra brought up some points, but I did not have a pen to note them down. At that moment, he told me that in the Army, an officer must always carry a watch, a pen, and a pocket notebook. Since that day, I have always carried a pen and paper with me, even during personal visits. It is amusing to now see people beg, borrow, steal a pen when they have an urgent need for it.

During the first few years in any job, it is wise to learn as much as possible on the job. It is important for an employee to maintain a diary or a log to write down the learnings for each day, particularly when ramping up on a new job. If there is an extended period with no new learnings, it would imply there is something incorrect with the employee's approach to the job, or that the employer is not creating the right learning opportunities for the employee, or both. The employee should take this up with the manager to discuss remedial measures or consider a different job if there is no resolution. There are many who have worked for years in a company just stagnating and learning nothing. Their youth is gone, and they become unfit for employment elsewhere, highlighting the necessity of constant introspection and striving to be in an environment that is conducive to learning.

Learning should not be confined to only what is within one's comfort zone or area of work. It should extend beyond the boundaries created for oneself. One of my training assignments was to spend two months in the accounts department. At Bata, cash was deposited locally in collection accounts for all the 1,200 stores the company had in India. The cash was transferred periodically to the head office account. Banks were not regular in transferring proceeds and frequently waited to bunch proceeds and deducted transfer charges causing delays and making reconciliation of accounts all the more difficult. At one time, over Rs 55 lakhs was outstanding in a suspense account. As the trainee, my assignment was to trace the transfer amounts. I took on the initial set of tasks in the accounts department with some reluctance, as I was a Marketing person, not an Accounts person.

Sensing my reluctance, the manager under whom I was a trainee called me and told me I was making a mistake in not using an opportunity to learn new things, even if they were not relevant at that particular point in time. I did the assignment and got so interested in Finance that I was motivated to enroll in British Institutes for a correspondence course in accounting. Over the years, this has stood me in good stead and has helped me develop a strong understanding and appreciation of financial matters. I succeeded in the assignment of tracing the transfer amounts. For the company, this resulted in a drastic reduction in loss by way of interest costs.

CHAPTER FIVE

Good communication

In all walks of life, there are brilliant people who do not have good communication skills. We have seen teachers and professors unable to establish a rapport with their students only because of their poor communication skills. Worthy candidates fail to impress interviewers and do not get selected for jobs. There are geniuses who simply cannot express their thought processes and share the knowledge they have.

The training in Bata honed our communication skills. Mr. Reginald and his assistant, Mr. Rao, were excellent trainers and had come up from the ranks. They knew every aspect of the sales operation and had good communication skills. They prepared meticulously for their lectures and gave assignments that kept us on our feet the whole day. We were told that communication should be clear and almost telegraphic in the use of words. Many readers will not forget the days of no phones, when telegrams were sent from the post office and when one had to pay for every word above the minimum allowed.

There was this intelligent endeavor to convey maximum content with minimal use of words. Readers will also remember that, at times, this economy of words would result in some severe misunderstandings at the receiving end.

Thanks to constant mentoring from our seniors, we were able to write crisp notes with the exact amount of information that needed to be conveyed. There was an Englishman called Mr. Hammond, who was the CFO. He called me one day and said that I should present my work to Mr. Bata, who was visiting India. This was an unforeseen chance and a test of my presentation skills. We did not have PowerPoint presentations and had to work with a viewgraph machine and transparencies. If lady luck was not on one's side, the bulb would fail in the middle of a presentation, much to everyone's embarrassment.

Communication skills took a real test later when I was working with Tata international, which was then under the Chairmanship of Mr. Nani Palkhivala. He was a very busy man, and it was indeed very difficult to get project reports approved by him. We had to make sure that the executive summary was very interesting to read and would catch his attention. If the summary was well written and promised to be useful, he would read the project report. Otherwise, it was rejected, and an opportunity was lost for the manager. We wrote summaries, which though brief, were all encompassing, and these were checked and rechecked so that no important detail of the project was left out. We had to anticipate the questions he would ask and have answers for them in the summary. It was also important to put down very clearly, the assumptions in the project and also the downside risks. This enabled us to see where we had gone wrong and take preventive action.

Many presenters do not pay enough attention to the summary. The top executives receiving the report do not have time to read the whole report and either read only the summary or get their assistants to do a short write up on the project. The latter may not have the nearly the same knowhow or motivation compared to the authors of the report.

Communication has to be authentic and understandable. The Army specializes in various types of training, including that of communication. When the Army is not actively involved in war, they spend all their time training, improving strategy, and building capability for wartime operations. An army officer is trained to not only give appropriate verbal orders to the jawan under him but also to get the jawan to repeat the order. This is done to check that the jawan has understood the instructions correctly. With a gun in hand, unless instructions are very clear, the jawan may fire in the wrong direction. During every briefing, the jawan is asked if there are any doubts, and he is encouraged to get clarifications before going ahead with the instructions so that there is no scope for error.

Mr. Prem Seth, who was my boss at Tata Exports in Delhi, taught me that a message, once written, should be reread to check that the message was conveyed correctly. Will the message convey to the other party what one really wanted to say? One had to read the message again with a role reversal, as though it was the receiving party reading it.

The following anecdote by a salesman who accompanied me when on a trip to Boston in 1978 will amply illustrate the disastrous consequences of incorrect messages.

In 1978, I was in the US on a marketing trip. I went to Boston and nearby places to meet some customers. I was accompanied by a salesman from our agent's office, reputed to be the 'crème de la crème' of all salesmen. This gentleman told me that he worked with Sears. A buyer in Sears had placed an order for 12,000 pairs of women's shoes with an Italian supplier. His secretary made a typing error and put an extra zero, making the order for 120,000 pairs. The mistake went unnoticed until large shipments started arriving. The buyer was shocked and in grave danger of losing his job. The buyer sent an SOS to this star salesman saying that he would be obliged for life if helped out of this mess. The salesman took up this job and actually sold the 120,000 pairs in two years. The buyer's relief can well be imagined.

It would be in order to digress and write about why this salesman was successful. Though Sears could very well have absorbed the losses had the shoes remained unsold, the salesman had salvaged an embarrassing situation. He built a permanent relationship with Sears and got preferential treatment. This gentleman was earning more than a million dollars per year in 1978 and did not want any promotions. I was curious to know how he managed to do so well when others did not even earn one-tenth of his salary. He took me to his house and showed me how he organized his work. He had several suitcases and when a customer called, he would check his notes and only take samples that were relevant to the customer. His rapport with his customers was so good that he could call any of them and get an appointment on that very day, while people like me might have to wait for several days.

Some communication blunders happened as a result of language barriers, as people translated from one language to another. While many were not costly, there were the occasional ones that provided for comic relief.

This is a true incident about a district manager of a leading shoe company who was asked to visit a store in Uttar Pradesh, and speak to the lady owning the premises about possibilities of extending the area of the shop. He was to request the lady to rent out an extra portion at the back of the shop. The lady declined. This was his message to the head office: "Landlady not willing to lend her backside, but I am trying hard and hope to succeed by tomorrow". His manager sent the following reply: "Do not waste your time with the Landlady's backside. Return to sales headquarters immediately".

At a particular shop was a man who was responsible for window display. He was very artistic and adept at decorating shop windows. The attractive windows got in more customers, and this immediately helped increase sales in the store. His job was to teach the store staff how to display merchandise in the shop window. The shop window was a prime source of attracting the attention of customers and its décor was changed periodically. This man always did a good job and would always report a sharp increase in sales. However, on one trip to Assam, he was not successful, and this was the telegram he sent: "Cholera Epidemic here. People dying like hot cakes".

Good communication also means prompt and relevant responses to incoming letters and, in today's context, mails. The Bata organization spent a lot of time researching current communication mechanisms to identify opportunities to improve and ensure timely responses.

The findings were formalized and resulted in rules that all employees had to follow. For example, when writing a letter, employees were asked to draw a vertical line dividing into two the A4 sized paper we used. The left side of the paper had to be used for the written matter. The right side of the page was left blank. These letters had the original and two copies in addition. The original and one copy was sent to the receiver. The receiver sent his reply on the right side of the A4 page and dispatched the original back to the sender. Both parties filed their copies in an orderly fashion. This correspondence file helped identify letters that had not been replied to. It would take just a few minutes for perusal. Moreover, it was also easy to see if a reply was relevant to the issues highlighted in the sent letter. Work was highly simplified and easy to control.

During my training period in Bata, Mr. Thomas Bata, the Chairman of the group, visited India. This was always a major event, and months of preparation went into these visits. His wife was a very good architect and had a keen eye for detail. Together, they visited factories, stores, and other projects in the company. Whenever Mr. Bata visited the sales office, he would go around some of the departments and shake hands with people. During such visits, he would invariably stop at an officer's desk and open the drawer to see the papers kept there. If there were letters unanswered or if the drawer had clutter or personal effects, all hell would break loose.

During my stint in Bata, there was much to be learnt from Mr. Ganesan, a Regional Manager for the South of India. He was meticulous in his work and had the reputation of replying to all letters the same day. He hired a personal typist whom he paid from his own pocket to help him in this task. When in Tata, Mr. Seth asked us to make sure that our replies addressed every point raised by the customer.

Great achievers hold communication as an important asset. When I worked with UNIDO, Mr. Sahasranaman, an IAS officer of the J & K cadre, was the National Programme Manager, and I worked very closely with him. He was very organized in his work, and his commitment was total. Within hours of every meeting, he would personally draw up the minutes of the meeting and send them across to all the participants.

Through clear communication, expectation setting, and follow ups, he ensured that all targets in the programme were met in a timely manner. I learnt a lot from him and admired his ability to simplify complex issues and find practical solutions. He was an expert at building consensus amongst a very diverse group.

At Bata, we were taught to make optimum use of the phone. In those days, the telephone system was quite primitive. Landlines were few and far between. The existing connections would be out of order for several days. On receiving a call, one should be all ears for what the caller had to say. One should air one's views only after the caller had finished. This may seem like a very trivial issue, but a little introspection will show that many of us are guilty of interrupting and being in a hurry to counteract. It does not require much analysis to realize that such actions completely disrupt the chain of thought of the caller. Compare this with others, who use the office phone for all their personal chats. Important files gather dust while the telephone line is blocked for all-important calls. Who is to tell them that such habits hold up crucial matters and have very far-reaching and detrimental consequences? I am also amazed at people who start forwarding messages on 'WhatsApp' as soon as they reach their workplace. What a colossal waste of time and energy!

The training in Bata prevents me from indulging in frivolous talk on the phone. My calls seem very abrupt to the person at the other end. I come to the point straight away without frills and diplomacies.

Going hand in hand with communication are ingenious strategies that great managers deploy in order to achieve their goals.

CHAPTER SIX

Strategy

Strategy has long been a tool that humans have employed to achieve specific outcomes. Great Indian epics such as the Ramayana and Mahabharata talk at length about the strategies employed by the characters to outwit the opponent. Strategy is commonly and routinely applied at home. Books on how to handle your children abound with advice, such as this one "When you want your children to do what you want, give them three options. Let the best option be yours."

Fathers have handed over their salaries to their children, asking them to manage the finances of the household to stop them from constantly complaining about their needs not being met. Two urchins, each selling knickknacks, in Bombay's local trains had this conversation when they met each other at the platform. One asked the other, in Marathi, "How much do you sell these items for?". The other replied nonchalantly, "Oh, I look at the customer and decide." This little boy had developed his own strategy of gauging the economic status of the customers and charging them accordingly. Managing a company needs good and appropriate strategy at all levels.

Here is a true story of a Japanese company that made clocks with an inbuilt alarm system. They wanted to expand their operations in the Middle East and sent a small team to study the market. This team found that stores there stocked the world's best brands of clocks and were not keen on the Japanese ones. As they delved deeper to understand the middle east market, they realized that what woke a typical Arab in the morning were the prayers called 'Adhan' from the nearby mosque. That sparked an idea that got them an inroad into the middle east market. The team got the most popular voice in the Middle East to record the 'Adhan' and used this as the alarm ringtone for their clocks. Very soon, everyone wanted to have one of these Japanese clocks even though they already had several others. The clocks were a great success. This company was intelligent enough to create an interest in its product and then went about delivering what became a highly successful product.

Today, companies like Apple have sold millions of their products even though such products never existed before, and nobody felt the need for them. The products catered to fancies and interests and were truly unique. Google and Facebook have gone one step further by offering services free to the customer and collecting the revenue through advertising or very specialized services like GSuite. Just as we attract a child with what catches its fancy, so too it is with sales and marketing. Identifying the current interests and fancies of the customers is a strategy.

During my training period in Bata, I was in charge of a large store in Kempegowda Circle, Bangalore. I was to temporarily replace the manager who had a brain tumour and was on leave for two months. This was a very large store, and I had to make sure that targets were met. Although I was doing well, the Regional Manager paid a surprise visit and reprimanded me for not doing more for marketing promotions. I asked him for advice on how to go about it. He said I should light up the store and have music playing for an entire week. This suggestion seemed to jar my sensibilities, and I conveyed my apprehension on this being a viable strategy. It was also my job to listen and obey, so I had Hindi and Kannada film music blaring the whole day, and the shop scintillated at night. To my surprise, the sales went up by 30%. Music and lights created a very festive atmosphere and attracted customers, even when there was no offer of a discount. I was also able to sell most of my old stock at a discount. I had learnt a good lesson from an outstanding regional manager V R Ganesan.

Another strategy that was successful in Bata was the use of colour coding to enable easy identification, as many sales employees were migrants and not highly educated. Shoe style numbers on the box label were printed in blue one year, green the next year, and red the following year. A person could walk into a store and immediately spot stock that was a year old and stock that was two years old. The company, as a policy, did not keep stock older than two years and if there was unsold stock, these were discounted and put aside for immediate clearance. Later, as a District Manager, I could go to any store, ask for all stock that was two years old. The lineup of the footwear would just take a few minutes, thanks to the colour coding. I could then check the quality and set prices at a discount for fast clearance of the stock.

Sales data at the store level and company level were also colour-coded. For example, estimates were always in red, achievements were in blue, and the previous year's figures were in green. This system was to be followed meticulously every week. Any deviation meant that the sheet would be shredded and trashed. A new sheet had to be prepared with the correct colour code.

I started as a shop helper in 1971. For three days, I was required to unpack and dispatch shoes and arrange stock. The stock in any Bata store is arranged in a sequence, which is exactly as per the stock statement for the store. A well-trained person can go to a Bata store anywhere in the world and be able to find a particular style in less than a minute. Within a particular style, stock is arranged size-wise for easy access. Excess stock is kept on the top rack or in the rear portion of the shop. Slow moving stock is kept in a particular rack to enable sales personnel to find them easily and show them to customers.

In the days that followed, I was assigned to be a salesman in a large store for a period of two weeks. This gave me insights on how to deal with customers and how to win a sale. The company expected better feedback from customers when a trainee dealt with them. Working in a retail store also taught us to identify genuine customers who came with an aim to buy and others who came just for window shopping. Gauging a customer was an interesting exercise in studying human behavior. There was also much experience to be gained. There were subtle strategies we learnt in dealing with customers. Let me relate an example. It is common practice, especially in the south of India, for a bridegroom to be given a pair of shoes and 'chappals' by the bride's family. When we saw a marriage party in the shop, we would highlight the most expensive shoes, playing on the psychology that only the best was bought for a wedding.

At times, much to my surprise, a reverse strategy worked. In later years when I was a District Manager, I visited a store in Meerut. A large number of customers come from villages around Meerut. The salesman there did not deal with pleasantries. 'Take it or leave it' is what he said to a customer. I felt this was rude and spoke to the salesman. He was very experienced and told me that the villagers only understood this type of language. Politeness would not work here. Sadly, I found this to be true.

There have been lessons in strategy all through my career. I faced many challenges in the UNIDO assignment that I took on many years later. I was to source international experts for various programmes and get them to come to Noida and work for short periods in The Footwear Design and Development Institute (FDDI). While we had guidelines under the programme for their remuneration, we had to handle cases where the person had excellent credentials and wanted a higher package. Mr. A Sinha, the Managing Director of the Institute, told me one day not to bargain on the rates and instead increase the assigned work so that they delivered full value to the institute. This strategy worked very well to the satisfaction of all. The institute published near 200 manuals on various aspects of footwear manufacturing in a little over three years. This was only possible because we were able to source talent from all over the world and get them to document best practices in a structured manner. The experts were given very precise terms of reference, and it was ensured that the work met the standard required. They also trained Indian counterparts so that the work would carry on even after they left. FDDI is today an Institute of National Importance.

In another instance, during my time at the FDDI, we received information that the State Trading Corporation (STC) had imported a large number of sewing machines and other equipment for footwear manufacturing, and that these were lying idle and in a state of disrepair. STC was also facing challenges with storing these machines, some of which were more than fifteen years old. Mr. A Sinha, the Managing Director of FDDI, negotiated with them and got these machines free of cost. We repaired these machines and were able to meet the requirement at the institute. As for the surplus machines, I suggested to the MD that we could rent these to small scale units and collect a small rental. The rental could be used for maintenance of the machines retained by FDDI. He approved of the idea, and we started renting out machines to small scale units for whom an imported machine was a welcome accessory and a major boost to their facility. Mr. Sinha had been the deputy CEO of Noida Authority and knew most of the units in the area. He said that we would just have an informal agreement with each person renting a machine. In case someone defaulted, he said he would personally go to the unit and pick up the machine and ensure that no one cheated FDDI. He was well known in Noida, and this simple threat was enough for the units to comply. Strategic leadership plays a big role in uplifting industry. Without the use of elaborate agreements and legal processes, we were able to render good service and put all the machines to use.

When I joined Sri City towards the latter part of my career, I was pleasantly surprised to learn that the Chairman Mr.Srini Raju, and the Managing Director Mr. Ravi Reddy had studied and lived in the USA for many years and had imbibed the US culture as far as customer satisfaction was concerned. They ensured from the word go that Sri City was always customer focused and friendly. This strategy of treating the customer as all-important has helped the company grow to the heights it has reached today. In the initial years of the company, Mr. Ravi Reddy personally met all customers to know their requirements and made sure that these were incorporated in the infrastructure decisions and policies.

Sri City did not advertise in newspapers or electronic media to attract customers. The marketing strategy was the personal interaction with potential customers and satisfying existing customers so that they spread the good word about the company and gave good references. Positive customer feedback is very good advertisement for a company and attracts customers who in turn make their decisions based on the good experiences of those already working with the company. Additionally, Sri City paid great emphasis on the quality of its presentations to customers, ensuring these were factual and addressed key customer concerns. Mr. Ravi Reddy, in particular, was a stickler in this regard, and the presentations went through several iterations before they were finalized. The audio-visual showcasing of what Sri City had to offer was highly rated amongst customers and served as a benchmark for others in this space. To expand reach across a broad range of customers worldwide, the audio was translated into several languages.

Another strategy that Sri City employed was to give cogent answers to questions customers asked frequently. Based on discussions with customers during the first five years since inception, Sri City had very extensive documentation as frequently asked questions (FAQs). This was the best in the industry and available in multiple languages. A customer was handed over an edition in the language of his preference. The document answered ninety five percent of the questions customers raised. The FAQs also categorized what the company could do for the customer and what it was not capable of doing. The FAQs document standardized the marketing pitch, which previously was different and inconsistent across various Business Development Managers.

During my tenure in Sri City, I introduced a unique feature by way of an internal FAQ as I found it impractical to get the team of marketing managers together for formal training. Every Sunday, I mailed a set of five questions to each team member. Answers to these questions required in-depth knowledge on various issues raised by our customers. The marketing managers were required to mail me their answers by the evening of the following Friday. I went through the answers and corrected most of them. On Sunday morning, I sent them the model answers so that they could see for themselves what the correct answer was and update their own knowledge. This exercise went on for about seven months, and at the end of it, we had a book of about 250 questions and the model answers. The marketing managers could refer to them when required. They all felt that they had gained significantly from this exercise and the marketing pitch was also more consistent. Whenever a new person joined, they were given this book, enabling them to ramp up quickly and build subject matter knowledge. There was a constant endeavour to stay ahead of the other companies. One of the more considerable outcomes of these practices has been that our marketing staff are well regarded by customers for their knowledge and sought after in the industry.

Sri City always followed the policy of promising less and delivering more to the customer, thus surprising the customer pleasantly. Commitments, though carefully made, were delivered meticulously. This was in contrast to what happens in most real estate companies and industrial parks in India. The developer and the customer are usually at loggerheads when the customer takes over and begins operations. Sri City has not had a single court case or arbitration with the customer in the last ten years. This was a big plus point for new customers. During discussions with customers, Mr. Ravi Reddy was always in favour of the customer, irrespective of the cost involved. Sri City always emphasized that they would stand by every word in the agreement and implemented this completely.

It is important that in any marketing department, the managers need to ask in what way their strategies are better than that of their competitors. I found that small companies could do this better than large ones because they were more flexible, and changes were easy to implement. These few examples are only to highlight the role played by good, simple, innovative strategies in a progressive company. Almost every function in an organization involves various factors, including strategy. One cannot isolate the strategy part. In some cases, it is the strategy that plays the lead role.

Very often, strategy involves catching a bull by its horns, especially when it deals with situations where ethics have been flouted.

CHAPTER SEVEN

Integrity

Integrity is a word that is all encompassing, especially when applied to business practices. From start to finish, it becomes an essential part of every process and transaction when an organization is committed to maintaining the highest levels of integrity. Unfortunately in today's times, integrity is slowly losing it's relevance, in thought, word, and deed. Malpractices have become so much the order of the day, that they do not seem wrong anymore. Be it greasing the palms of a clerk in a government office, or underhanding dealings in transactions or money laundering - there is a collective loss in conscience and desensitization in today's society, that ethics are rarely a source of bother or consideration.

During our first week as trainees in Bata, the training manager,

Mr. Reginald told us that discrepancies in financial matters would be taken very seriously. Every person suspected of having caused that discrepancy would be considered guilty unless proven otherwise. This was contrary to common law, where a person is innocent unless proved guilty. This meant that if we submitted travel or other bills without supporting vouchers, it would be assumed that we had fudged the bills and hence could not produce the vouchers. As a result, the culture of carefully preserving all vouchers and attaching them with our claims, was inculcated in us. I have carried on this practice even today, and my bills have rarely been queried. These methods helped us maintain high standards of integrity. Sadly, presenting inflated bills seems to be a norm these days, and integrity is often a value system of the past.

The next step in our training was to manage three stores, each in a different state of India. The training manager would pick stores that had poor sales, personnel issues, shortages, or large number of staff. The reason for choosing different states was to acquaint us with the rules of octroi duty and sales tax rules. Managing the stores also meant that we had to achieve the targets set for the store.

In my very first assignment at Secunderabad, I was asked to resolve the problem of large shortages in the shop. It was obvious that some staff members were stealing from the shop. The shortages were more than the contingency allowance of 0.25 % of the turnover. The shortages above the contingency had to be borne by the manager. This would mean a big hole in my pocket, which was something I could ill afford. In the very first fortnight, I had a shortage of Rs 125, which was about 20 % of my monthly salary.

This was a problem I had to solve myself. After all, I did not want to hand over my salary to thieves. I called the staff and told them that I did not come to this store to pay shortages, and if I caught anybody, I would make sure that they had the harshest punishment, including a jail term. I also devised methods to do frequent and random checks of stock. I would leave the shop for lunch or tea at different times. Sometimes I would be back in five minutes and at other times in twenty minutes. I also stood unnoticed, at the street opposite the store, to see what was happening. My batchmate Vikas Toley was in a store nearby, and I asked him to stand in for me at times. The staff was unnerved, and the shortage stopped. Surprisingly, two weeks later, when I was ill with jaundice and away from the shop for three days, there was no shortage. I had solved the problem and also learned how to fix store shortages.

Mr. Ganesan, my regional manager at that time, had a phenomenal knowledge of stocks, bestsellers (not books but footwear), and sales promotion. He knew every store in his region like the back of his hand. His method was to visit the stores frequently and get firsthand information on all store related issues and resolve them. If he made a commitment, he made sure it was kept. He checked all aspects of the Bangalore store, where I was posted, but could not find fault. He even checked the cash. Since I was new and did not want any shortages discovered during surprise visits, I had kept my salary in the store locker as an exigency. When Mr. Ganesan saw this, he told me to keep my personal affairs separate from that of the company for good control.

Bata was one of the first companies in India where no sale was made without a cash memo. Prices were fixed, and bargaining was not possible. Therefore, sales tax and other dues to the Government were correctly accounted for and paid to the last paise. Everyone knew that in a Bata store, it would not be possible to avoid sales tax. The company had set an example for compliance, many years ahead of other large companies. Sales tax inspectors could rarely find fault and harass the company staff.

Employee provident fund data was eventually computerized, and provident fund dues were paid promptly. In many organisations, employees have to literally wear away their shoes running around for money rightfully due to them.

In Bata, there was a tradition that the Managing Director would attend the farewell function of every officer in the company. An Englishman, Mr. Gordon Thring, was the Managing Director, and he came to attend the farewell function of a junior officer. This officer had some financial difficulties and requested the Managing Director to help him get his dues quickly as he had no other income except his settlement money. The Managing Director assured him that he would try his best to help.

The next morning, Mr. Thring issued a circular to the finance department saying that if they wanted him to attend a farewell function, he would do so only if the final settlement cheque for the employee was ready for handing over at the function. From that day, all employees got their dues on the last day of service, saving employees a lot of hassle.

Simple instructions can result in major changes in the way an organization works. Being fair in one's dealings has to work both ways. Employees have to be fair to the company they work for, and vice versa. When being fair is only one sided, there is a lot of discontent which greatly affects many areas in one way or the other.

In 1984, I was already in Tata for four years. The Dewas tannery had a serious problem of losses and this could not be arrested despite several changes in strategy. Mr. Syamal Gupta had just joined as the Managing Director. He had earlier worked with Tata precision industries in Singapore. The tannery was losing Rupees Hundred thousand per day. He studied the problem and found that none in the company could solve the profitability issue. He immediately looked outside India to find a suitable person for the job. This was very unusual at that time. In about two months, they found an Englishman, Mr. G Pearson, who was interviewed and found suitable. He had worked in a sole leather tannery and did not have experience in upper and lining leathers that were made in Dewas. The tannery was also selling a lot of leather to Russia. The volume of sales was very high, but the business was very tricky and unprofessional. After the production of leather, there was a wait of several days for a Russian inspector to arrive and clear the goods. The inspectors were very whimsical and expected to be wined and dined and be given generous gifts in order to clear consignments. These expensive pleasantries were not in the company's rule book and huge stocks were held up owing to delay in inspections and rejection of stock on flimsy grounds.

Mr. Syamal Gupta took a bold decision to get out of the Russian business, even if this meant a large drop in sales for the company. In the end, even though margins were low, everybody realized that this action was good for the company.

Mr. Pearson's contribution was that he rationalised the purchase of raw material and ensured that the tannery operated at full capacity. At the same time the marketing organisation was revamped to ensure that the products produced were sold in proportion to the grades that were produced.

Disciplinary action is very often a tricky business. In Bata, we were also taught how to handle shop staff and take disciplinary action when necessary. We were instructed on the modalities of conducting domestic enquiries and types of disciplinary action that could be taken. Training involved issuance of charge sheets, suspension, domestic enquiries and dismissal orders that would stand court scrutiny later.

There was one case in Meerut, where I had charge sheeted a salesman. He went to a labour court, claiming that he never got the charge sheet. I was able to show details of the registered letter sent by me and also details of his having acknowledged the letter. The salesman did not deny this, but said that he had only received an empty envelope. From that time, I made it a point to file charges on an Inland letter. The envelope was done away with and so too the excuse that the charge sheet was never received.

There are many HR managers today who are not able to issue proper charge sheets and conduct domestic enquiries in a manner that will stand any legal test. Small mistakes can cause great harm to a company's case. For example, a person is sometimes suspended without a charge sheet and an enquiry, violating the principles of natural justice.

More than fifteen years down the line, when I was with Tata Exports at Dewas, Mr. Viren Mehrotra, the General Manager suspected that an employee was stealing expensive material belonging to the company. He collected evidence and one day, when the company bus left the factory, he allowed the bus to cross the gate and stopped it a few yards outside the gate. The person was caught red handed. Had the bus not crossed the gate, the employee might have claimed that he was only shifting material inside the factory and did not steal. It was foresight and acumen on the part of the General Manager.

Verdicts in a labour court generally tilt in favour of the labour force. Many companies today do not document all unacceptable codes of conduct. They also do not put down in writing the punishment for any unacceptable behavior. Once offences and corresponding punishments are put down in black and white, every employee is clearly aware of company policy. Chances of controversy and the need to take issues to court get largely reduced.

When the Tata Dewas factory was being built under the Chairmanship of Mr. Moolgaonkar, a boiler was installed and had to mandatorily undergo inspection and certification by a government inspector. The boiler was built to specifications that had been approved, but the inspector did not clear it and was delaying the project. It was obvious he wanted his palms greased.

When Mr. Moolgaokar was informed about this, he asked the engineers to check the boiler again and ordered that if no fault was found, they should inform the Chief Secretary about the delay in the inspection report and approval. The engineers were also asked to add in their letter the fact that Mr. Moolgaonkar was displeased and annoyed. A senior officer was dispatched to check the boiler and it passed inspection. The message to the Chief Secretary was delivered. The inspector who expected a bribe was arrested and action taken against him. Mr. Moolgaokar was known for his integrity, and this enhanced the reputation of the company.

All those who held high positions in Tata in the early eighties, were simple men who were given a lot of freedom by Mr. J R D Tata and they did exceedingly well. Mr. Moolgaokar, who built Telco from scratch and was Chairman of several Tata companies, did not even own a flat in Mumbai when he retired. Mr. Russi Mody was the Managing Director of Tata Steel and yet he was able to connect with every worker on the shop floor. Mr. J R D Tata always said that the key to the success of Tata companies at that time was that he employed leaders who were smarter than him and whom he could take advice from.

During my 26 years with Tata Exports, we were always told not to fudge any documents or make false statements to the Government or other agencies. If taxes were not paid on time, the officer was held responsible. Tatas were known to be honest and ethical, and this reputation helped them considerably in several tricky situations.

Around the year 2000, when I was the Vice President of Tata International in Chennai, I had to sign several documents for customs. I would carefully check all documents before putting my signature. Over time, the custom officers recognized my signature and cleared consignments immediately. It was a matter of great pride for me, that my signature was valued by customs officials and this fact put a greater responsibility on me. Integrity was one of the core values of the company and was never compromised.

When I lived in Indore, there were several Tata officers who were also living in independent houses nearby. It was known that most of us did not have any great monetary assets. The joke was that if each of us put a board with his name, and 'Tata Exports' below it, in front of our respective homes, no thief would ever break in to steal, because there was very little to take away. There were several senior managers like Mr. Viren Mehrotra, the Head of the leather Division and Lt. General Malhotra, the Director, whose personal conduct was such that nobody could point a finger at them, on any matter. Both gentlemen included the families of the employees in all gatherings, and made people feel that they were part of a big Tata family.

Travel protocol

Whenever we travelled on tours to other units of the company in Bata, we had to get a travel authorization and the Asst. Sales Manager would only sign these at the last minute, after he had questioned us about the objective of the trip and whether we had taken all the required documents. On return from the trip, our report had to be submitted within 2 days and would be accepted only if minutes of discussions were signed by the person we met.

This simple rule avoided misunderstandings of any sort and ensured that all issues were discussed and resolved. This is a far cry from official travel becoming more of a pleasure trip.

Human goodness still prevails

During one of my surprise visits to an agency, in Khatauli, near Meerut, I found a large cash shortage and pointed this out. The agent admitted to being responsible for the shortage. I then issued him a charge sheet and started working on the means to recover the money. I did not realize the passage of time, and very soon, it was late evening. Khatauli was a very small place and did not have any hotels or restaurants. I had to go back to Meerut. The agent told me that the last bus had already left at 5 PM and I would have to wait till morning for the next one. I tried to get a taxi, but there was none. I had no choice but to accept the offer of the agent to stay at his place. Khatauli is a very notorious place. I had had a tough day with the agent and had fired him and issued a charge sheet. Now I was staying in his house and really feared for my life. I hardly slept the whole night. The next morning, I left as soon as the first bus was available. I appreciated the agent who gave me dinner and accommodated me in his house. He was also good enough to pay back the shortage amount in the next two weeks.

Handling the workforce

During my days at Tata Exports, the culture was to treat all workers, staff, and management with respect, and people took pride in working for the group. We rarely heard of cases of sexual harassment in any of our companies, and if at all any wrongdoing happened, the response was quick and exemplary. I have known cases where some very good employees were caught in issues that involved integrity. In all these cases, the offenders were dismissed. This set a very good precedent in the company and made clear to the employees that nobody could get away with improper dealings and unethical behavior. Food was served in the canteen, where workers, staff, and officers ate the same food on the same table.

This helped avoid a lot of complaints about the quality of food.

Managers in Tata companies were expected to make sure that relations with the labour force were cordial, and 'go slows' and 'strikes' were avoided. The larger group companies like Tata Steel and Telco had provided excellent examples of not having any major disruptions for several years. During my tenure, we had a large number of dedicated contract suppliers, and it was our responsibility to ensure that these units paid wages on time, and all legal dues were paid correctly. There was rarely a case where matters went upto the labour commissioner or other officials. I found that if senior managers kept good contact with workers and listened to issues raised by them, workers would have confidence that the management was fair and would address their concerns. I did not have any strike over five years, and the main reason was that we addressed all the small issues without delay. These related to drinking water, harassment by security, cleanliness etc., and were very reasonable issues. Once these were addressed on time, they did not create major problems when it came to larger issues like wage increase. Good communication, fulfilling commitments, and being fair was the key to a peaceful relationship. Many HR managers fail to understand this and drag their feet even on small issues causing workers to get angry. For example, if a worker wanted a salary advance due to a genuine emergency, the rule book could easily be relaxed and the money given immediately. We had a cap of two months salary as the maximum for such advances. We tried to ensure that in genuine cases advances were paid within twenty four hours.

The other problem I have found is that many HR staff do not ensure that company rules and policies are explained clearly to the staff. What behaviour or action is acceptable and what is not acceptable has to be clearly spelt out. Also important is to make the staff aware of punishments that correspond to every rule that is broken. For example, if stealing is considered a major offence, then every employee should know that punishment is dismissal irrespective of the amount stolen. If this rule is applied impartially to all, including officers, the number of such cases falls drastically. We were told that mistakes would be accepted if they were genuine and not a repeat of earlier mistakes. On the other hand, corruption or unethical practices would result in immediate dismissal.

Tata code of conduct

Many companies have unwritten rules on how employees should conduct themselves while dealing with other stakeholders. Since they are not written down in black and white, interpretations vary, resulting in inconsistencies in the way issues are dealt with. Tata group was amongst the first to introduce a written code of conduct called the Tata code of conduct.

This booklet made it clear that the core values of a company would not be compromised under any circumstance. The core values were clearly defined. The document also listed the do's and dont's with regard to gifts, awarding contracts, recusing oneself if there was conflict of interest or declaring any conflict of interest upfront. It is not easy to compile such a document, but the Tata group did it, and many managers found this to be very useful for their personal conduct and also when we had issues relating to disciplinary action. Employees also agreed with the rules since they were stated up front and not devised on a case-by-case basis.

CHAPTER EIGHT

Customer Relations & Achieving Excellence

Man is a social being. In that capacity, he has to interact with other human beings. Experience and observation will show that, in general, successful people are those who know the art of handling people and handling situations calmly and wisely. I have been intrigued by the ways in which people need to be handled to achieve the desired outcome. Some were very contrary to my own views.

Companies like Bata, Tata Exports, FDDI Noida, and Sri City, owed their success to the efforts of the people heading them, and for whom the customer was all important.

In Bata, the company took complaints very seriously. If a

customer was dissatisfied with the merchandise, they could get a replacement in a Bata store anywhere in India. Merchandise rejected was shipped back to the claims department of the concerned factory. The defective products were analysed thoroughly and the cause of the complaints identified. The collated data provided very useful information to the production department and corrections were immediately made. This process, though expensive, was worth the time and money spent on account of the insights it provided about the quality of products manufactured. Once a week, the factory manager would go to the claims department and acquire firsthand knowledge of issues involving the quality of products.

Whenever a customer gave a written complaint, the matter went to the Regional Manager who ensured that the complaint was resolved to the satisfaction of the customer. Category merchandisers also brought very valuable feedback from customers and this was very carefully evaluated and acted upon. Today most retailers buy footwear from suppliers and whenever there is a problem, they replace the shoe and debit the supplier. The whole process has become mechanical, and less customer oriented.

In the seventies, Bata was one of the top five famous and admired brands in India. Every time Mr. Bata came to India, he would visit some retail stores and he always made sure that he served a customer personally and ensured that the customer had a happy experience.

In any shopping cetner or market, the store manager of a Bata store used to be highly respected, a person customers trusted. Mr. Rattan Kumar, the manager of the Bata store in Connaught Place, Delhi, was the most customer friendly manager I have known. The store was the highest selling store in India. Mr. Rattan Kumar was always at the store entrance welcoming customers. They included ministers, bureaucrats, ambassadors, and other important people. He knew many of them personally and I have seen many VIP customers specially ask for him. They would readily buy the shoes recommended by him.

Today store managers in retail shops rarely have a great rapport with the customer. They are usually inside the office and not supervising the operations on the shop floor. A good manager can make a world of a difference to the way a store performs. More than thirty years after Mr. Rattan Kumar retired, people still remember him for his service. Bata Connaught Place has never been the same since he retired.

Here is an experience with a difference. It almost falls in with the Sanskrit phrase 'Sama Dana Bheda Dandopaya'. Found in Hindu epics, this suggests various ways to sort out a problem and find a solution. Starting from talks, going on to gifts, then logic and strategy, and finally war.

Tata Exports was a very customer focused company thanks to Mr. Tata, Mr. Moolgaokar and the Managing Director. If any customer had a complaint, they almost always sided with the customer. The person concerned with the sales would be taken to task, if there was a complaint that was not attended to or not properly resolved.

One of the key selling points of Tata was that if a complaint warranted it, a person from India would fly out to the complaining party, gauge the problem, and settle the issue amicably.

Mr. D'cruz was the Marketing head for leather at Dewas. The factory had supplied white leather to a customer in Australia. The customer complained that the leather had turned yellow on arrival and was not really white. Mr. D'cruz flew to Australia, and on finding that the complaint was justified got the shipment returned to India.

The company policy was that if there was a complaint, it should be attended to immediately. If goods were found defective, the material had to be removed from the premises of the customer. It is a very bad policy for companies to leave defective goods with the customer as it is a constant reminder of a bad supplier, and this tarnishes the image of the supplier further.

Tata Exports had acquired a good reputation for not cheating any customer. The company could make genuine mistakes due to lack of knowledge, hidden defects, or inability to understand the customer requirement fully. However, they never tried to cheat the customer or resort to excuses. Any executive trying to indulge in unethical practices would be sacked if found guilty.

Sri City, for whom I am working at present, has very clear cut guidelines for handling customer visits. This covers customer care from the time the customer reaches Chennai to the time of departure. Chauffeured vehicles are provided from and to the airport. The round trip is around four hours. Lunch, coffee, tea, and snacks are on the house. In fact, the excellent lunch is a talked about feature among the customers. They always look forward to lunch during their subsequent visits. This sort of hospitality is a big relief to the customers as the site is very large in area, far away from the airport and going to a good restaurant would be time and energy consuming. The strain of the long drive and the site visit around the campus which takes about two hours is much reduced on account of this generous hospitality. In the larger scenario, this may seem trivial, but it is attention to such trivialities that goes a long way into building good customer relationships.

Among those who visited Sri City, there were representatives of many Micro, Small and Medium Enterprises (MSME) from Japan, Italy, Spain and a few other countries. They found it difficult to find a good architect and other personnel to construct their factories in conformity with their customized specifications. We had one Spanish customer called EURA who had got a quote of Rs 40 Million for their factory. When the matter came to me I did feel that the quote was quite inflated. The customer also said that this cost was higher than what he would pay in Spain. After analyzing the demand and a calculation of cost involved we offered to build them the factory true to their specifications for Rs 18 Million. This was inclusive of a 15% fee for our services. The customer gave us the contract and we did the work with transparency and delivered at the promised cost. They were very happy and have been our supporters since then.

Many industrial parks feel that once they sell or lease the land, their responsibility towards the customer is done with and that it is the customers' job to take care of all ensuing problems. Sri City had a different approach. The company would provide all required support in order to be able to put up a factory in 6-8 months. This time was the international norm. We at Sricity felt that handing over the the land was only 25 percent of the job. The remaining 75 percent would be in the form of customer support. Towards this end, we gave customers all the information they needed and guided them through the approval process so that they did not have any problems. None of the 187 companies in Sri City have paid penalties for non-compliance on account of not knowing the rules or incorrect interpretation of rules. This attitude really differentiated us from other parks and we soon became the favoured destination.

Most of the large industrial parks in India work on getting an anchor customer who would in turn bring in many more customers or suppliers. This customer is given the advantage of acquiring land at a price lower than the cost price. We decided not to follow this policy, as we were a multi product park, and an anchor customer would favour only a particular sector. We did not want too many customers in the same sector and in a down turn become another Detroit. This policy proved to be very successful and we were able to get a wide range of customers including many Fortune 500 companies and global leaders in many sectors.

I have always admired Ferrari cars for their market focus. Ferrari is an iconic brand known all over the world. They only make about 8000 to 9000 cars per year. The waiting period for a car is fifteen to eighteen months. Every car is produced only on order. The fact that demand for their cars increases with increase in pricing speaks volumes about the company. Ferrari does limited advertising, has enormous pricing power, and is a brand that exceeds customer expectations year after year.

Many companies employ consultants but rarely write up clear terms of reference and delivery standards. The consultants are under utilized and the companies invariably blame the consultant. Companies also fail to allot a counterpart full time to learn from the consultant and implement projects. Another problem is that even when consultants make suggestions, they are not implemented. Companies should only employ consultants if they are willing to listen to them and implement what they suggest. Consultants can always be questioned if the implementation does not work. There is no use of employing a consultant, if their suggestions are questioned and not implemented. A lot of money is spent without commensurate results.

One of the assignments that I was given was to set up a world class physical testing laboratory for footwear and allied materials in the FDDI. I was required to do this in just a few months. I was fortunate to be able to visit some of the best testing laboratories in Bally, Switzerland and PFI in Germany. They are world class laboratories, with staff having decades of experience. During one visit, I was to buy a weighing scale from Mettler. I found the price to be very high and asked why one had to pay so much when good balances, made by Avery and some other companies were available in India. The Lab Director smiled and took me to a laboratory balance. He then asked me for my ball pen and weighed it. He then gave me a piece of paper and asked me to draw a straight line one inch long. After this he weighed the ball pen again. To my surprise and disbelief it showed a lesser weight.The balance was sensitive enough to register the small amount of ink used up. The lab Director then asked me if the Indian scale could match this. I immediately agreed to buy the Mettler scale. Later I found that most jewelry shops today use the Mettler scale for precision weighing.

Subsequently, I met the Secretary of Industry, Government of India, who assured me that I would be given a free hand on purchases, on the condition that I delivered a world class testing laboratory. I told him that if I went by the lowest price tender, I would never be able to buy equipment like the Mettler scale. He understood my dilemma and said I need not base my decisions on the price factor and he would give his approval for purchase requests. He kept his word and we were able to set up one of the best laboratories, using state of the art equipment, in a short span of time.

The accuracy of any testing lab depends on the quality of equipment, the testing method and the interpretation of results. This needs to be documented and checked regularly for compliance. We had negotiated with PFI, Germany for collaboration and the agreement provided us with all testing methods and interpretation methodology. We also had access to the latest research in PFI. This was thanks to Mr. A Sinha who negotiated hard with PFI Germany to get access, at any time, to all the research done at PFI Germany. This was a great help and enabled FDDI to establish itself as a premier lab in India.

We kept record of all samples tested and sent them frequently to Germany for cross testing to ensure that our results tallied with theirs. This helped ensure standardization, predictability and repeatability. Industry accepted our reports and we were able to justify our test results at all times.

Setting up the lab was quite a challenge. The premises was on rent, and we had to ensure a fixed temperature of 20 degrees at constant humidity, throughout the year. In those days, air conditioning equipment was not well developed in India. We had to work very closely with Blue Star to ensure that we achieved the required parameters and maintained it. Our young staff was sent to Germany to train in testing methodologies. They were good learners, did very well, and became experts in a short period of time.

FDDI established very good training systems experts from world over, who spent a lot of time in India and were very good in their work. Every lecture was well planned and the whole syllabus was covered methodically. Tests were conducted regularly to assess the students.

As the Director Technical, I would hold surprise tests to ensure that the syllabus was being taught properly and the students were able to assimilate what was taught. The first few batches of students did exceedingly well and many are now CEOs of large companies. The industry also held in high esteem the quality training, and willingly recruited FDDI students.

I have written about learning experiences and managerial goals. I repeat, it is very difficult and maybe almost impossible to compartmentalise values, skills, and learnings that a good manager needs to have. What is needed is a blend of these things where each attribute surfaces in a certain proportion as and when the need arises. What better example than Rama of the famous Ramayana. He was an 'uttama purusha'. He had various roles to play and excelled in each by showing those qualities that were needed most for that role.

Let me now talk about the great managers I came across during my career and how their personalities and stories made an everlasting impact on me.

CHAPTER NINE

Leadership

Good leadership is motivational, inspiring, and educational.

During my training period at Bata, we had a strike by the clerical staff in our sales headquarters at Kolkata. Strikes were quite common in Kolkata in those days and we were used to disruptions. Mr. Seth, the Sales Manager at that time, got all the management trainees to take on all the clerical work so that company operations would not be disrupted.

This definitely meant extra work. Each one of us spent about twelve hours per day at the office. It was quite amazing that a bunch of about 35 trainees and officers could run the business for almost three weeks, without the help of the 'babus' (clerical staff).

Mr. Seth would ensure that we got an allowance for each day of extra work so that we could end it with a good dinner.

This assignment helped us learn many jobs at the lower level and understand them better. Such an understanding stands in good stead for a manager when it comes to controlling the people working for him or her. It was also a lesson in self-reliance.

In 1977, I was posted to the export department in Kolkata. I had worked a little more than a year as a District Manager in Dehradun and was quite happy to continue. The sales manager, Mr. V K Lamba (he later became the Managing Director) wanted me in Kolkata. Export was considered a prestigious posting, and I accepted. One day, I went to meet Mr. V K Lamba for some approvals. After the approvals were over, I suddenly remembered that there was another problem I needed to sort out, and I asked for his opinion. He knew that I did not have any suggestions of my own. Instead of readily giving me a solution, he advised me to think about ways in which I could sort out the problem. It was only then that he would do one of the following: a) accept the solution, b) modify the solution, c) come forward with his own solution. This was a very important management lesson, and from that time onwards, I never went to my boss to discuss a problem unless I had a solution of my own. Today many young managers do not apply their mind to a problem and simply seek solutions elsewhere.

A company's standing can be judged by the way its offices and factories are maintained. A shabby work area is never conducive to efficient performance. Lack of aesthetics also has far reaching consequences. Mr. Bata was a stickler and would forgive no lapse on this front. Whenever his visit was announced, there would be a major drive to remove all junk in the office and in desks. Several kilos of paper were discarded. All letters were answered, and decisions were taken on time, and the organization was shipshape before such visits. The offices looked clean and fresh.

We were housed in an old building in Kolkata, and during every visit a few layers of paint were added to the walls. The joke was that you could tell the number of visits of Mr. Bata by the thickness of the paint. The Czech Managers would visit an office or warehouse and pick a shoebox at random and surprise of surprises, only that shoe would have defects. This was despite the fact that managers took great pains to ensure that everything was checked and inspected before such visits. This uncanny ability of the managers kept people on pins. Mr. Josef Vyoral was one such Managing Director, and I used to marvel at his ability to spot a mistake even when the sample size was very large.

Mr. Bata was very incisive in his remarks, and though he did not speak very much, every comment was worth studying and evaluating. During one visit, while discussing retail store profitability, he asked about rentals being paid and was told that the company had long term (15 years) agreements and the costs were below current market prices. He immediately asked the head of retail to conduct a study and find out if the company was making profits on real estate or from the shoe business. He asked for profitability figures, taking into consideration market prices for rent. We had never done this exercise before, and the results were revealing. Many stores were making profits because of lower rent and not on account of the business. This was told to me personally by Mr. Bata. For a company, what is important is not just profits, but how exactly these profits come about. McDonald's USA has several fast food outlets. However, not many know that they are amongst the largest real estate owners in the US. Today 64 percent of their profits come from rentals, and they own USD 39 billion worth of real estate. They charge franchisees 8-15% rent when the normal rent is only 6-12%. The rent is also assured.

Time is crucial for a good manager, and there is little time for discussions with a person who has requested an appointment and not prepared well for discussions. I once had an appointment with the managing director. I needed his approval on prices. I met him, and in ten minutes, the prices were discussed and approved. At the end of the meeting, I remembered that I had another issue to be discussed. I asked for permission to present the problem but he refused, saying that I had not mentioned this in the appointment request. He told me nicely that I should organize my work better and come fully prepared next time. Though I was taken aback, I learnt a good lesson. After this incident, whenever I went to meet very senior people, I always went prepared with all relevant papers and the meetings invariably went well.

On another occasion, I had a meeting with Mr. Duteil, who at that time was the Technical Director. He was French and a man of few words. He strongly felt that if a person worked sincerely, there was no need to work after office hours. In fact, if anyone stayed late, he wanted an explanation as to why they could not finish the work on time. This was valuable learning for young managers.

Learning to let go is something that most people in Senior management need to adopt.

I believe that in a company where professionals are employed, a Managing Director should not work for more than ten years. This period is sufficient for the individual to drive change and produce results. After ten years, fatigue sets in, and yes men begin to play a major role. Here is an interesting anecdote.

Dr. Irani was an iconic Managing Director of Tata steel, who steered the company through a difficult period. On the last working day prior to his retirement, he called his secretary and asked for a screwdriver. He then personally unscrewed his nameplate and took it with him. He told his curious staff that he was doing this in order to ensure that the nameplate did not remain there one more day than necessary. He did not want the functioning of the new Managing Director to be stifled by the nameplate of the previous Managing Director.

In early 1980, I joined Tata Exports as Marketing Manager for the footwear division and was based in Delhi. Tata had applied and got a license to set up a large tannery in Dewas, Madhya Pradesh, and the footwear division was set up in order to use the leather from the tannery to make shoe uppers and shoes that were exported subsequently. The tannery was set up in 1975 and the footwear division was established a couple of years later.

The tannery project was set up on a plot of hundred acres, adjacent to the National Highway linking Indore to Bhopal and Agra. The project was the brainchild of Mr. Brij Nehru, the then Managing Director, and Mr. Sumant Moolgaokar, who was the Chairman of the company.

Mr. Moolgaokar was a visionary and had already set up TELCO in Pune. This was the first unit in India for the manufacture of trucks. It took several years to build this factory, which ultimately laid a strong foundation for business in trucks. It is said that once when Mr. J R D Tata met Pt. Jawaharlal Nehru, he was asked why it was taking so long to set up the factory. Mr. Tata replied that Mr. Moolgaokar was setting up an industry and not a factory. It was an enormous task to build a supplier base and a 'sales cum service' network in India when none existed previously.

The Chairman, Mr. Moolgaokar, was a great environmentalist, and his passions were trees, water harvesting, and water storage. When construction of the factory started, he had pillars built at fixed points in the campus for photographs to be taken. Every month the project manager had to send him six photographs from the same positions as those taken in the previous month. In Mumbai, Mr. Moolgaokar's secretary would then place the six photographs of the previous month, along with the six photographs of the current month. If the photographs showed that the planted trees had not grown, he would immediately question the project manager and hold him responsible. This was a very simple and effective method of checking on how the trees were growing on the campus and also on how construction was progressing, without any reports being submitted. Compare this with the delay in projects being caused by mounds of paperwork unattended to.

After Mr. Moolgaokar retired, Mr. Nani Palkhivala, the renowned lawyer, became the Chairman. He was a giant in the legal world, and his analysis of the annual budget brought thousands to the Brabourne stadium in Mumbai. His simplicity belied his phenomenal knowledge. I had the opportunity of being his 'aide de camp' when he visited the factory at Dewas and spent a full day with him. I asked him how he was able to make such brilliant speeches, all over the country on varied subjects, and whether he had many assistants who wrote his speeches. He told me that he spoke extempore and spent about ten minutes of quiet time thinking about the subject of the lecture. He was able to organize his thoughts sequentially, and the rest followed. His English and diction were unmatched, and even when he spoke in the Supreme Court, all judges listened very carefully to his arguments. His strength was his ability to absorb all details of complex issues, simplify, and give practical solutions.

During one of the meetings in Dewas with Mr. Palkhivala, the agenda was an important issue relating to land owned by the company. Out of the 182 acres of land allotted for the leather project, the company had used only 100 acres, and the Government was pushing for the use of the remaining land. The lease rent was very low, and the sale of grass from this land was sufficient to pay for the lease rent. When someone suggested that we could perhaps sell the land, Mr. Palkiwala became angry and said that he would never agree to a sale of the land during his tenure. "Land was ten years profit," he said. The meaning was that the value of the land at any time was equivalent to the profits that the company would make in ten years. How could we just give away a prized asset when there was no pressing need for the cash at that time. I will always remember this statement because many companies have sold their best assets to show short term gains and lost out in the long run. Companies like Bombay Dyeing and Godrej had prime land available in Mumbai and did not sell when their manufacturing activity declined. In the next few decades, they gradually monetized the land and gave substantial gains to the stakeholders.

Great personalities like His Holiness the Dalai Lama, whom I had the good fortune to meet, are classic examples of people who remain calm and compassionate whatever be the circumstance. Mr. Palkhivala was also a person who rarely lost his temper. After observing him and also other senior directors of the Tata group, I realised that these people were in these positions because of their qualities. Keeping one's cool and not losing one's temper was an essential requisite to being a good manager. Mr. Syamal Gupta, who assumed chairmanship later, rarely lost his temper, even under the most provocative of circumstances.

The tannery in Dewas used to buy goat and cow raw material, which came in about ten grades based on quality. Each grade was a certain percentage of the total pack and was the raw material for different products. The marketing department usually sold the top three grades easily, and this accounted for only 30% of the raw material. The other unsold grades of raw material accumulated and resulted in huge stocks.

At other times, there was a reversal. The lower grades got sold quickly, but the top grades remained unsold, resulting in high inventory levels and underutilization of tannery capacity. As mentioned earlier, it was the Chairman Mr. Syamal Gupta who appointed Mr. Pearson to sort out the problem of huge losses in the Dewas tannery. Soon after joining, Mr. Pearson set out to motivate the staff. He identified all the problems, checked on the daily inputs and outputs and ensured that the tannery was working to full capacity. He then reorganized the marketing so that all grades got sold at the same time and inventory levels came down. Losses were gradually replaced by profits.

This was not an easy task and required very careful planning and pricing to move all the stock profitably. In conclusion, it was Mr. Syamal Gupta's foresight in hiring an outsider and Mr. Pearson's ability to completely reorganize a system and get the same set of people to adapt to it, that was responsible for restoring profitability.

This learning experience I brought to practice several years later, while working at The Footwear Design and Development Institute in Noida. We used a large number of foreign experts who did outstanding work to take the institute from infancy to an institution of national importance.

In late 1992, while I was working at Tata Exports in Dewas (Madhya Pradesh), we had a visitor called Mr. Amarendra Sinha. He was a young IAS officer and had recently been appointed as the Managing Director of the FDDI (Footwear Design and Development Institute). He did not have much knowledge about footwear at that time and visited our factory to see and get a feel of the operations. I did not know him, but during the visit, we struck a rapport with each other. At the end of the second day of his visit, he asked me if I would join him at the FDDI as the first Technical Director. I was surprised and said that it would be difficult for me to work for the Government with a reduction in salary. He told me that the United Nations Industrial Development Organisation (UNIDO) was giving aid to India and could employ me. They were looking for a person from the industry who could implement the UNIDO programme to develop the FDDI.

Despite this, I was still hesitant, but Mr. Sinha's insistence made me attend a selection interview in Chennai. I did well and was selected for the job. Mr. Sinha then spoke to my boss in Tata, Lt. Gen S L Malhotra, who was our Deputy Managing Director. He readily agreed to release me as I would be working for the country. In fact, he took up my case and got me a special lien, which would enable me to return to Tata after three years. This was indeed a great gesture from the Managing Director, Mr. Syamal Gupta. I was to have a tax free, well paid job with UNIDO. Since I could come back to Tata, there was job security too.

Initially, my assignment was for three years. At the beginning of each year, I was given a work plan with clear targets and corresponding deadlines. At the end of that year, a group of foreign experts audited my programme, reviewed my contract, and based on their report, my tenure would be extended for another year. I got five extensions before I returned to Tata in 1998.

One of the challenges in the UN job was that I was given a budget to spend, and my performance was based on my ability to spend the money and complete the projects on time. In all the jobs I had in the past, I was taught to save money, but here I had to spend money to retain my job.

FDDI in Noida was a training, testing, and consultancy service provider to the footwear Industry. The Ministry of Commerce, Delhi, was responsible for its inception. Mr. V Balaraman, the Managing Director of Ponds India, was appointed as the Chairman. Coming from the private sector, he was very customer focused. He knew most of the senior members of the Industry in India. If at all there was a complaint from any customer of FDDI, he would immediately take this up with the Managing Director, Mr. Sinha, who was also customer focused. He not only sided with the customer if there was a dispute but also made sure that the complaint was resolved immediately.

It is to their credit that FDDI had the best customer ratings for their training programmes, and for their testing and consultancy services. They were on par with good companies, where practices were concerned. The common misconceptions that people had about government organizations were proved false. FDDI was far ahead of other private organisations where customer focus and satisfaction was concerned.

Due credit needs to be given to a fair and strict Mr. Balaraman and Mr. Sinha, both of whom, in a matter of just two or three years, ensured that the operations of FDDI were always transparent and free of corruption or nepotism.

When we started the consultancy business in FDDI, everybody was very skeptical about a government organization being successful. With Mr. Balaraman and Mr. Sinha we devised a simple system. Our expert would visit the customer and take up the work. At the end of the assignment, we would mail the MD of the organization to determine whether or not he or she was satisfied with the work. If the MD was not satisfied, we asked for the areas of deficiency, and accepted the MD's word. Our expert was required to continue with the assignment, without additional payment, till the deficiencies were sorted out, irrespective of how long it would take.

Thus, our staff members were under pressure to ensure that the work was done well and if there were extensions, they would not be paid for this, and this would reflect on their performance. The customers were very satisfied with this system and gave us more assignments and also paid on time.

In early 1990s, the Indian leather industry had a serious problem when the western world laid standards for PCP (pentachlorophenol) at 6 PPM (Parts per million). Our industry was not ready for this and also did not have testing facilities in India. The issue was also political. European countries had a standard of 6 PPM when the supply was from India and from the far east countries. However, for supply from France, 50 PPM was acceptable. When a material is carcinogenic, how could we have different standards?

Dr. T Ramasami, who was the Director of CLRI at that time, quickly studied the whole issue and helped the industry move away from PCP. They also established test facilities in India. The most important contribution from CLRI was that they were able to prove that the testing in Europe was not consistent and that the method itself was faulty. This gave us time to catch up and resolve the issue. Having our own strength in India was a great boon for the industry.

Board Approvals in FDDI

The FDDI was under the Ministry of Commerce and had a board consisting of government representatives and industry leaders. They had almost a dozen members and getting proposals approved was not an easy task. Mr. Sinha would prepare the agenda and circulate it to members. Two days before the board meet, he would personally go and meet the board members and explain the proposals and get their tacit approval. In case there were too many vehement objections, he would simply drop the proposal. This system satisfied many of the board members who felt happy that he went to meet them and take their help. The board meetings were very smooth.

The private sector could use these strategies too. Sometimes CEOs have great difficulty getting proposals approved at board meetings. Building a consensus before any board meeting is crucial for smooth functioning of any organization.

CHAPTER TEN

Artisan Projects at FDDI

In 1996, the National Leather Development Programme had the agenda of providing technical knowhow to footwear artisans in the country thus ensuring their livelihood. The aim was to give them simple inputs, which could standardise their production and help them add more value to their products and thereby survive the onslaught of the organized sector.

All over the world artisan products are sold at a high premium because they are unique, one of a kind and involve manual labour. The products are not assembly line churned out by machines.

A machine cannot replicate an artisan's work. It is only in India that artisan products are sold at a great discount. Khadi, Mojari shoes, Kolhapuri chappals and similar products are hand made and sold at discounted prices. In the textile sector, companies like Fab India and Kalamkari have provided the design inputs and technology, thus improving the products and adding value. The footwear industry, till then, did not have such a scheme.

The biggest problem with artisans in Delhi, Agra and Jaipur was that they were using wooden lasts or forms to make footwear. These were cheap and easy to procure. The difficulty was that the wood was not seasoned, and of poor quality. It expanded in summer and contracted in winter. The dimensions from one pair to another varied widely and it was not possible to sell them as standardized products. The lasts were also not based on good fit and aesthetic design and devalued the product. The artisan could not use standard footwear components like insoles and soles due to this dimensional inaccuracy.

In a very ambitious programme, NLDP decided to develop plastic lasts in the various production units across the country and provide them at the price of wooden lasts. The lasts were very carefully developed with the help of experts. Bata was considered the best for good fitting lasts since they had done elaborate surveys and decided on the correct fit for men and women shoes. However, Bata had not updated their database and used 25 year old data. We were able to do dip stick surveys and spoke to several artisan units and developed lasts which were much better in fit than the Bata lasts. These lasts not only helped standardize fit for artisan shoes but also gave them a chance to make standardized footwear.

The programme involved a huge subsidy of almost Rs 250 per pair of lasts. This was after we had negotiated a very good price with the last makers, who were now getting bulk orders. Over 50,000 to

60,000 pairs of lasts were produced and distributed to artisans, enabling them to move away from inaccurate wooden lasts. This has helped them to survive and compete with the organised industry. During my visits to these artisans after 20 years, I was very happy to see that they not only survived, but prospered and were making good money.

The NLDP programme then moved further to provide good design inputs and materials to artisans. We invited top Italian designers to come and train our Indian designers, and they did so for a small fee. Earlier, the only option was to go abroad to study design. This was very expensive and was only possible through sponsorships by organized companies. Now, even small units could avail of the training in India. Many young designers benefitted from this and subsequently did very well for themselves. We had these Italian designers teach and also make collections of shoes with corresponding lasts and patterns, which were then given at highly subsidized rates to artisan units. This helped them improve the quality of their shoes. The fact that they used plastic lasts helped them use standard components like insoles and soles. They could not use these earlier due to dimensional changes from pair to pair in wooden lasts.

The biggest beneficiaries of this programme were from Karolbagh and other areas of Delhi and Jaipur. In today's market, I see some excellent Mojaris made with good components and lasts. The industry is now flourishing. It was an enjoyable experience meeting artisans, visiting their units, and understanding their needs. Our job was to fulfill these needs. We were greatly helped in this project by Dr Schmel from UNIDO Vienna and Mr Timo Nicolas Salminen from Finland. They were very passionate about this project and provided great help to augment support for our programme. Concerted team effort helped us realize our goals and also help thousands of uneducated people survive in their trade. Kolhapuri chappals also improved immensely in design and fit with the NLDP inputs. The fact that they have survived for over twenty years after the programme, clearly indicates that the NLDP programme helped such artisans with its useful inputs, guiding these artisans to better methods of production and a brighter future as a consequence.

Testing

In the early nineties, footwear testing in India was in it's infancy. The equipment available was meagre and there was not enough rigour in the testing and subsequent interpretation. The final analysis was not consistent and meaningful.

At that time there were two leading laboratories for footwear testing. One was Satra (Shoe and allied Trades Research Association) in the UK and the other was PFI in Pirmasens Germany. Both the labs had done many years of testing and were highly rated for their equipment and test reports. Bally Switzerland also had a very good lab and I had the good fortune to spend some time there as a trainee.

During my term at FDDI, we studied these labs and the NLDP programme. Under the leadership of Mr A Sinha, Dr Schmel and Mr Sahasranaman, we decided to have collaborations between these labs and the Indian Institutions. The Central Leather Research Institute collaborated with Satra UK and FDDI collaborated with PFI Germany. This in turn led to acknowledging the deficiencies in the Indian Laboratories that did not allow them to be top grade.

As an example, the Indian laboratories did not have the right equipment for testing. Much of existing equipment were outdated and not calibrated regularly.

Through this process, we became acutely aware of the requirements for a laboratory of repute:

- Good Equipment
- Standardised methods of testing
- Documentation for interpreting results
- Counter testing to check the validity of our reports
- Regular calibration of equipment
- Trained personnel to do testing
- Stable laboratory conditions like temperature and Humidity
- Replicability of test results in other labs

The agreement with PFI Germany gave us access to all their data and our staff trained in Germany and India for skills in testing. We recruited some Post Graduates from IIT Delhi. They held M.Tech degrees, were smart, quick on the uptake and soon established the credibility of the laboratories. Initially, many International companies did not trust the accuracy of our laboratory, but when we proved that the counter tests in Germany gave the same results and were validated by PFI, the customers accepted our reports. The fact that we preserved samples for six months helped us repeat a test if required, and recheck the results. While many laboratories in India did not have these systems in place, it was very satisfying to know that the upgradation of the laboratory in FDDI was worth the effort and money spent. Now testing of Footwear and allied products could be done in India.

CHAPTER ELEVEN

Managerial Policies

What should companies do if they want good performance from their managers?

1. Have a good training programme.

2. Give additional emphasis to the annual assessment to all the managers responsible for conducting training programmes.

3. Expose the employees to challenging situations in the company, where they apply their minds, learn from peers, seniors, and juniors.

4. Mentorship.

I have had the good fortune of having mentors throughout my career. Mentors are experienced colleagues who take an interest in your welfare, guide, and advise you. One learnt a great deal from mentors.

Many a time, the best ideas come from workers or junior employees, and we should learn to carefully listen to them and implement their ideas. At one time, Toyota Japan had nearly 3000 suggestions per employee per year, and they made great progress implementing them and later became the top car manufacturer in the world.

Computer literacy is a must.

Today, computers have become a necessity in almost every sphere of life. Back in those days, when mainframe computers were just making an entry into the business world, it was loud and clear that computers were here to stay. Not only that, computers were not a luxury but a necessity.

In 1971, there were only a handful of companies in India that had computers. Mr. Bata had invested in IBM, USA, and was a Director in IBM. He had understood the importance of computers and had many of his companies use these computers. We, at Bata India in Calcutta, had a fairly large computer, and this was housed in an office in Camac street. This office was next to the IBM office and was chosen such that its proximity to IBM Kolkata would make maintenance easy. The computer was used to process all stock statements fortnightly, production plans, payrolls, and Financial data.

As compared to other companies, Bata was proactive and used computers for its vast operations that spread over 1,200 retail stores and 14,000 wholesalers, with 500 lines of merchandise. Doing the same job manually would have been a stupendous task.

I used to visit the computer centre often and had developed a good relationship with the Manager, Mr. Roy. He once told me that he was having difficulty in reconciling the stock from the large number of stores and lines of shoes at the year end. As a solution, it was decided that a dummy data entry would be made to balance the stock. This, of course, would not appear in the printed version. In those days, auditors were not trained or aware of doing system integrity checks and accepted the stock statements. The dummy entry was of a small value and did not have any material effect on the financial results of the company.

What was the learning outcome? In any computer programme, it is very important to check its integrity and have controls to periodically evaluate them.

Many years later, I went to the International Institute of Information technology (IIIT), Hyderabad. I was shown a programme that translated from English to an Indian regional language. However, when the same sentence was translated back to English, the result was not the same.

Data that has been entered in Excel cannot be trusted because there is scope for alteration of the data without attracting notice. Many companies use Excel without realizing this and have suffered due to manipulation by some employees or outsiders.

Unfortunately, with the arrival of computers, mentorship, and personal interaction with colleagues and shop floor employees has diminished considerably. People now send emails from one table to the next, rather than talk to each other.

Moreover, emails always make people cautious because it is in black and white. Resolving an issue by email may be more complicated than just walking across and verbally sorting out the issue.

Drawbacks notwithstanding, companies need to keep themselves updated on computer technologies and upgrade their systems and training programmes. Asian paints in India is considered to be one of the world's best users of SAP software and have been able to consistently make higher profits than their competitors. They do not have distributors and deliver paints to dealers thrice a day.

Need to be organized

In the early seventies, while we had computers, we never had software like Excel. A lot of correspondence was manual. Bata had a standard tabular sheet that looked like an Excel sheet. Data was entered manually on this sheet, with the tool being widely used for computing all statistics like production, sales figures, profits, analytics, etc. The orderly way of entering data proved very useful.

In my narrative, I have mentioned time and again, the need for being organized in thought, word and deed. This is life's lesson and not just confined to the world of managers.

Human resources

Bata had a good system for the evaluation of officers, and this was largely performance based. There was one interesting document called the passport to promotion, which was a passbook given to officers. Whenever an officer was promoted, the passbook was updated, and the job requirements for the next higher position was also listed. The employee's capabilities were also listed. It was now possible to identify, right at the onset, the skills that the employee needed to acquire in order to reach the next grade. Very few companies do this elaborate exercise to help the employee identify skillsets that need to be acquired or strengthened.

What is a better option? Appraising a disappointed employee of the lack of skills that led to missing a promotion, or motivating them to build the expected skill sets right in the beginning, so as to set them up for success for future promotions?

The higher a person goes up the managerial ladder, the more important it is to delegate jobs to subordinates, and concentrate on issues where they can add most value. The job of a Managing Director is to develop and deploy strategy for the company. He or she needs to take board approval for allocating resources. It is not the Managing Director's job to monitor travel expenses, freight bills, credit extensions for customers, etc.

'The perils of constancy' is another issue that I would like to place under the category of human resources.

Bata had a rule that all officers must take their annual leave.

People who did not take their leave were not rated highly because they most probably had skeletons in their cupboards that they did not want to expose. Else, they considered themselves indispensable and had not trained anyone to take over.

It is very important for every company to clearly identify sensitive positions in purchase, finance, stores, and HR and make sure that the officers go on leave for at least two to three weeks every year and that the position is manned by a substitute during this period. This is one of the effective ways to prevent fraud. Frequent transfers every two or three years is also beneficial. Many frauds have occurred in companies because the same person held a position for several years and built a coterie of yes men under him. A recent example is the Rs 12,000 crore fraud in Punjab National Bank. The concerned officer was not transferred for several years, although the rules clearly mandated such transfers. The fraud was uncovered only after the officer was finally transferred.

On the positive side, when people went on leave, it gave substitutes an excellent opportunity to add to their skills.

Companies need to give brownie points to Managers who identify and train substitutes. The assessment procedure should include this aspect.

A company should not make itself susceptible to blackmail.

In my later years, when I was President of a company, we had a person who had been trained to do some critical work. The company was growing and did not have too many people. One day, this employee came to me and said he was quitting because the salary was low. I had to accept this argument because his work was critical, and we gave him the raise. Immediately after, we trained another person to do this work. Six months later, the same employee came for another raise. This time we asked him to leave, and he was shocked. He never did well in the next few jobs that he took. Employees must learn that they cannot blackmail a company just because they are doing some critical work. Nobody is indispensable. At the same time, employers must be able to identify and retain high performers so that they do not lose talent.

In manufacturing companies, many highly skilled workers put the company in trouble when they take unauthorized leave at critical times. In such cases, the company must spend time and money to de-skill such operations, so that others can also do the same job easily. Another way is to provide incentives to operators to acquire skills for the operations of the stations before and after the operator. When an operator can man three positions, the smooth running of the entire production is possible even under untoward circumstances.

While hiring top level managers, a company needs to use discretion. Can a person with a string of degrees deliver the goods?

Graduates from Business schools go in for jobs with plum salaries. Once they get in, their work does not justify the fat pay cheque, and they are forced to leave and take another job. This then continues from one job to another. Leaving a job within two years is often an indiciation of an employee not being able to deliver goods. In some cases, the company does not give them the responsibility and challenges that were initially promised.

So let us take a look at top management selection. I would put this also in the category of Human resources.

During the seventies, most members of the Board of Bata were expatriates from various countries. They were selected from various Bata companies worldwide, and work in India was considered a challenging assignment because of the size and scale of operations. The process of selecting the Managing Director, Finance Director, and the Technical Director was very elaborate. In any year, only one new person was inducted to ensure continuity and smooth running. If a new managing Director was identified but was not very strong in finance, they would select a financial expert and place him in India a year earlier so that when the new Managing Director arrived, he had an expert to fall back on for advice. This was a complex process and implemented throughout the Bata organization as early as the seventies.

In the US, it is common for companies to get specialist Managing Directors at different stages of the organization. For example, if there was a major restructuring required, they would bring in a person with relevant experience to clean up the company and put things in order. In another case, a company doing reasonably well but not increasing sales at the pace required by the board, would bring in an expert in this area to work for two to three years to drive step change improvements. Once the growth stage was stabilized, they would bring in another person who only needed to steer the ship. This practice is not followed in many Indian companies but deserves looking into. For example, General Electric today is going through a major transformation, and CEO's have been replaced at least twice in the last three years.

In the early seventies, Tata Exports advertised for a chartered accountant. A person named Mr. Kaki Dadiseth was interviewed, but not found suitable. The same gentleman later became the Chairman of Hindustan Lever. This was clearly an error in not being able to spot great talent during the interview.

Risk analysis

Every company needs to analyse the risks involved in its functioning and adopt appropriate methods to tackle these risks.

In yet another study in Bata, it was found that over fifteen years, the Insurance premium for the large stock the company possessed in over 1,200 stores, was far greater than the loss due to damages. Hence it would be cheaper not to insure the stock. Diverse locations of the stores meant that potential damages would be localized and limited to a fraction of the total stock.

Risk assessments were very rare in those days. Today, it is important for all companies to do a comprehensive risk assessment and clearly identify the risks and the corresponding impact on the company. It is also possible to arrive at a 'value at risk' for a company and keep the board informed. In the companies I worked with subsequently, there was a rule that any claim from a customer could not exceed the value of goods sold. If this rule is not followed, many companies could sink due to one claim. When I worked for Tata Exports, the share capital was only INR 5 crores. Once, Nike USA wanted to buy footwear from the company, and their lawyers wanted unlimited claim provision. This included product liability as well as consequential damages like loss of profit, brand value erosion, etc. We asked Nike to quantify the claim amount so that we could take insurance in the UK and add this to the cost, but Nike wanted unlimited liability. We did not take the contract, and I feel this was a very good decision. A claim of one hundred crore rupees could have sunk the company. Nike lawyers asked us why we did not agree when smaller companies had readily accepted. We told them that a small company would simply wind up and start with another name the next day, whereas we could not do the same.

When I was President of an industrial infrastructure development company, we had a CEO from the USA who asked us what our investment was at that time. I told him it was about INR 250 crores. He said his investment was INR 600 crore and what would happen if our company sank. His loss would be more than ours. This was a difficult question to answer at that time, though subsequently our investment also increased substantially and protection measures for customers were introduced.

In 1979, I became the Export Controller for North America with Bata India. This was a very challenging job, and we had very demanding customers in Canada and the USA. We were required to see the Managing Director quite often since export prices had to be personally approved by him. The reason was that many times we had to sell with marginal profit in order to be competitive. Hence it was the Managing Director who decided on the prices, based on several factors like volume of orders and utilization of existing material from the tannery.

So far, I have tried to compartmentalize learning experiences and elaborated on each. But what really happens in the day to day working of a company and its employees is an integration of many factors, both positive and negative. It is essential to see the working in its entirety, analyse it, learn from it, and think of strategies that could cause an improvement in any sphere of activity.

CHAPTER TWELVE

My days at TATA

There are a lot of behind the scene strategies, and risk analyses that goes on before a company finally arrives on the business map.

Tata Exports (later renamed as Tata International) was an export company and was set up to promote exports of group company products as well as other products that were either manufactured or traded. The company was not listed, although many Tata companies were shareholders.

Export is a high risk business in any country. In the eighties and nineties, Tata Exports had to also contend with severe controls by the government.

No CEO of an export company can thump the table and say that their business will survive for more than ten years. The reason is that in the export business, there are several factors over which the company has no control, and this could sink the business overnight. Some of these factors are exchange rates, non-tariff barriers, quotas, political risks due to sanctions, or preferential treatment given to underdeveloped countries with duty exemption. In the early days, the company had understood the risks and decided that in spite of these risks, long term decisions had to be taken for this business. Therefore, the company was not listed, and shareholders did not expect constantly increasing returns every quarter.

The footwear business had potential, and there was good demand in Europe and the USA. The government also gave generous incentives to help exporters. With the rupee devaluing by 6-8 percent every year, cost increases could be absorbed. The net profit margins were only 6 to 10 percent. Every season the company had to prepare a collection of shoes and present them to large retailers like Walmart, Marks and Spencer, Clarks, etc. If the capacity of the factory was, let us say, 100,000 pairs per season, we would seek out four customers, each taking about 25,000 pairs. If the shoes did well, the business would grow to 120,000 pairs in one season, and this put a lot of pressure on the factory to deliver 20 to 40 percent more than normal output in that season. On the other hand, in a poor season, the output could fall to 80,000 pairs. Keeping a monthly paid workforce hit the profitability of the company. Companies in North India therefore adopted the piece rate system and got over this problem. In the eighties, orders were never a problem, but delivery on time was the big challenge. A delay of even two weeks would mean that we would have to airfreight the shoes at our cost. This killed profitability for the season. Over time the government incentives reduced, and the rupee became more stable as a currency. This led to a fall in profitability of the units in India. Many companies did not survive, while a few did well and expanded considerably. They were able to retain their customers and worked with them for several years.

The interesting thing about the footwear business was that all over the world, the manufacturing was mainly by small family owned units. The owners had control of all aspects of their production. The only exception was China, where companies had large capacities of about a million pairs a month and were able to control the business well. This started with the sports shoes business, where orders were given six months in advance, and there was enough time to procure raw materials and deliver on time. This extended to leather footwear in China. The Chinese had large sample rooms that could deliver ten times the number of samples that companies of other countries were capable of. They were also prompt in their deliveries. Indian companies did not have the capability to scale up quickly and remained small and became uneconomical in the long run.

Many large corporate houses like Hindustan Unilever, Tata, United Breweries, Sanmar, Wipro, etc., made entry into the footwear export business, but most of these major players, with the exception of Tata, have exited the business owing to low profitability and high risk. Entry barriers for this industry were also very low. This resulted in many new players entering the market, leading to intense competition. In the footwear business, an investment of Rs one crore, typically, could result in a turnover of Rs four crores, and with a 6 percent profitability, give a return of 24 percent on capital employed. This was possible only if capacity utilization was at least 80-85 percent and costing norms were adhered to by the manufacturing units. Delivery on time was also important since delays would result in goods being sent by air, and freight charges reduced the profitability considerably. In many companies, high stocks and nonmoving inventory caused the turnover to investment ratio to reduce. Obviously, this also caused a huge drop in profitability.

The footwear business requires quick decision making, and corporates were unable to do this as they had established procedures for capital expenditure and other investments in labour, etc. Decisions took time, and invariably, it would be too late. Based on fashion trends, some new machines could be required overnight. While small business houses could take a quick decision and move forward, corporates were limited in their ability to do so. The business volumes could be 80 percent of capacity in one month, and the next month would require 130-140 percent of capacity if orders were good. Corporates were unable to gear up so quickly. One method that we used with some success was to build in-house capacity to only 80 percent. Thus, even in the worst of times, the factory would be occupied. The next 20 percent was given to vendors who were given fixed wage costs in case capacity was not utilized. The extra 20 percent or more was given to transactional vendors who would, depending on their capacity, cater to the surplus in orders.

Selling shoes had been in the hands of family owned businesses but later was dominated by corporates like Nike, Adidas, and Reebok. They were able to develop new styles, engineer them, get them produced in China or other countries, and distribute them effectively.

An important lesson that I learnt at Tata was that in the export business, one should not commit for more than a year while booking contracts. One of the products Tata exported was rice. In the commodities division, the officers had enthusiastically booked orders for more than a year, at margins they thought were very good. Changes in the exchange rate and increase in prices of rice resulted in huge losses for the company. The company then made a rule that we could not book orders for more than a year unless specifically cleared by a committee, who then ensured that safety clauses were incorporated in the contract.

Promoting Excellence

When it came to the purchase of expensive capital equipment, managers had full freedom to look for the best and buy it. Chairman Mr. Syamal Gupta believed that the company should not buy yesterday's technology but look for tomorrow's technology. Managers took pains to study all aspects before buying machinery, and all were up to date on technology related to their respective fields. It was not necessary to buy at the lowest price, as long as we could justify our decision with facts and data. We spent several hours with Technical experts from suppliers to understand the special features of all machinery. Once the equipment was bought, it was expected that the machinery would be put to full use. Managers came in for heavy criticism, if there were reports to the contrary.

In the footwear business, we had to make designs that were up to date with fashion in the markets we exported to. On one visit to Italy, we were looking for new styles in Moccasin shoes, as producing such shoes was our strength. I went to many design studios where, for a price, one could buy a style along with corresponding patterns. Each set cost around 200-250 USD. In one studio, I was introduced to an Italian designer who was reputed to be the world's best designer for Moccasins. His price was around USD 350 for a style. I asked him what differentiated him from the others. He smiled and said that if we bought his patterns, we could straight away give the patterns for die making and go into production without having to test the patterns and make corrections where required. This saved a lot of time and money, and hence his price was high. We bought a couple of styles and what he said was indeed correct. Customers immediately liked the style, and this helped us in our sales. This designer only produced moccasins and did not work on any other type of shoes like boots and closed shoes.

Perfection yields immense results, and this passion for perfection needs to be developed by our Indian managers in everything that we do.

Every year there is a parade in Delhi on January 26, which is India's Republic day. This parade is watched by millions all over the world and is a symbol of the country's pride. The Army has the responsibility of conducting this parade. It is led by a Major General from Delhi. In such a large parade, we could always have mishaps like a tank stuck on the road or mistakes in the march past. If a tank stops midway, it would be impossible to clear it quickly, and the parade would have to stop. The Army Chief makes it clear to the Major General that he would have all the powers to conduct the parade, but one slip would be the end of his career. Preparations start three months in advance, and perfection is achieved every year. If we want to do it, everything is possible. The Republic day parade makes every Indian very proud, thanks to the impeccable arrangements made by the Army. No excuses are allowed or accepted.

I have also admired the Japanese companies for the way they plan and organize an event. Much time is spent and a lot of effort put in. The resulting perfection is evident. During any event, the front rows of seats are reserved and have the nameplates of important guests. Hostesses guide the guests to their seats. The role of each person in the company is clearly defined, and the result is an elegant and flawless event. For a meal, seating is predetermined with nameplates at every seat. In the invitation, guests has intimation about the table number allotted to them.

There is a lot to learn from the Japanese with regard to planning and execution. Even when they import large machines, the personnel in the logistics department take immense pains to check the routes, unloading, and installation protocol so that there is no error, delay, or damage to the machinery.

I had the opportunity of visiting the Huawei development centre in Beijing in 2016 along with Dr. Ajay Kumar IAS, who was Additional Secretary in the Department of Electronics, Delhi. The visit has been my best so far. The reception, the tour, and lunch, each was perfectly timed and organized. Every display panel had audio explaining the details. When we finished the tour of the development centre and came to the lunch table, the framed photographs of our visit were on each seat. All of us were amazed and inspired by the perfection the Chinese had achieved. It is no wonder that they are leaders in 5G technology, and this is worrying a lot of countries.

Handling People

When I was heading the Chennai office, I was asked to issue a dismissal letter to a staff member who had been indulging in union activities, causing difficulties for the company. The company was not against staff unions, but this person had crossed limits and had been transferred from Mumbai to my office as a punishment posting. When I received the termination letter to be issued to him, I called this gentleman and explained the reasons politely and told him that I had nothing personally against him but this was a company decision. To my surprise he accepted the letter without too much of anger and soon left the company. As a person, he was a good man and was well meaning and helpful to all in the office. It has been over 16 years since I left the company and I am happy to say that I am in touch with this gentleman as a friend and we hold no grudges against each other. If we are fair and straightforward in our actions, even the most difficult decisions will be accepted.

There was another case of a major union leader in Chennai who tried to organize our workers and raise fresh demands. We could not accept all the demands and also wanted commitments on increased productivity from the workers. One day, when the negotiations were not going anywhere, I met him alone and explained our position and that we were paying better than the market and had not defaulted on any payments. If he pushed his case too much, the operations would be unviable and we would have to close the operation. I also gave him a number of facts and figures. To my surprise, he agreed at the end and said that he would not press for new demands and the matter was settled amicably. It is not true that all union leaders are unreasonable and many like him understand genuine issues relating to the company. The most important thing is that they want to be treated with respect so that their image in the eyes of employees is good.

Cleanliness

Mr Prem Seth was a very meticulous person and was very organized in his work. He made sure that we came well prepared for meetings and also ensured that when we left the conference room, we put back all the chairs and had the room in good shape for the next meeting. These value systems are rarely practiced these days. A messy room, paper strewn on the floor, dusty tables, coffee cups lying all around, water bottles - are sights that do not jar the sensibilities of an employee. In India it is also the 'someone is there to do it' attitude that predominates. A lesser human being has to clear the mess made by a superior!

Dignity of labour is a lesson to be learnt.

CHAPTER THIRTEEN

Innovation

Every company needs to change with times and innovate in order to remain in the market. We have seen global companies that have collapsed because they did not innovate or change with time and necessity.

As an example, we can take Kodak Japan. With excellent quality, affordable prices, and an efficient distribution system, they were world leaders in photo films. Yet, they collapsed because they did not take seriously the impact of the digital revolution in films, and change their products. Competitors took over their market share very quickly, and they lost out.

Bata India was also market leader in footwear in India. When plastic footwear was introduced, they were the pioneers to introduce the 'Sandak' range in the seventies. This was readily accepted in the market because we had cheaper, washable footwear that met the needs of poor people. For several years Bata sold almost six to ten million pairs per year. They introduced 'injection moulded' footwear for the first time in India.

Many years later, Bata failed to recognize the importance of unit soles made of PVC, TPR, and Polyurethane, which made its entry into the market. With the arrival of unit soles, the whole production system changed. Uppers could be made at one place, soles at another, and the assembly into footwear could be at yet another place. Bata did not adopt the unit sole technology in the early years and continued to make all shoe components in one place, resulting in high costs. To add to its woes, many competitors came into the market and made shoes which were not only of good quality, but cheaper too.

In the seventies, Avery India held the monopoly for weighing scales. I had once applied for a Sales Manager's job in Kolkata because it was well paying, and they gave each sales manager a spanking new Bullet motorcycle. This was a big attraction for young men like me. During the interview, I was told that for every order of a platform scale, a twenty five percent advance was mandatory. It took them four years to deliver each order. Thus, the entire working capital was funded by advance payments from customers. Over the years, they were not able to maintain the lead over competitors who came into the market with weighing machines of good quality.

These examples show us that though running a business is

important, the way we do business is equally important. There has to be change to meet the challenges that time and customer requirements bring. Many companies fail to recognise this and do not incorporate meaningful strategies to change the way they do business. The railways introduced computers, and IRCTC, their subsidiary, brought about a revolution. Train tickets could be bought online. At present, over 500,000 tickets per day are issued online. They have brought about a paperless system where it is sufficient to show the ticket using your cell phone or any other electronic device. In fact, it is sufficient to state your PNR number, with the passenger having a valid identity proof. This is a remarkable example of how the customer experience can be changed for the better. In a country like India, with its huge population, the days of standing in a queue at reservation counters and poring over the reservation charts at the train station are over. This efficient, accurate, time saving system has saved the railways crores of rupees.

Companies need to spend time every year to systematically evaluate how they have changed the way they do business. A few years ago, brick and mortar retail stores felt that their sales strategies were the best, and they could face no threat. When companies like Amazon came into the market, they did not believe that these companies could revolutionise the business. Retailers felt that vegetables, clothes, and footwear could never be sold online, and customers had to feel and touch the products before they bought them. This has been proved wrong, and today even pharma products are delivered online. Bata will also have a serious challenge from online retail, and, unless they adapt quickly, they will be left behind in the rat race.

The strength of Bata lay in the fact that they ran their business in developing countries and specialised in manufacturing locally. Over the years, they have lost the manufacturing edge, and with large scale procurement, their strength is only in retail. If they do not catch up with online retail, they will soon lose this advantage and lose out to the competition. Their research and development efforts have also not caught up with time. For example, with respect to fit in shoes, the last survey was done more than 50 years ago but has not been comprehensively updated. When I was at the FDDI, we did a new survey and found that fit measurements had changed and we helped small scale manufacturers adapt to the change. These shoes are therefore as good, if not better than Bata in fit, and Bata is at a disadvantage.

I have learnt that unless a company has good metrics to measure various aspects of their business, they are not in a position to know their value and standing in the market and therefore cannot improve. Almost 50% of the metrics that Indian companies have are 'motherhood metrics'. This means that companies make assertions on the quality of their product without any measurements or monitoring methodology. A company feels that its product is good and the customers are happy. Where is the proof?

Every department of a company should have five or six carefully selected metrics that are easily measurable, repeatable, and predictable. They can then monitor their business and make changes when required. I have not seen a better company than Amazon for good metrics. The top management spends a lot of time reviewing the metrics themselves and the measurement systems for each metric. Amazon today is able to get sales figures worldwide by the hour throughout the year. How many companies can do this when the operations are spread globally? They employ highly qualified Ph.D. staff to develop and improve metrics. Amazon is next only to the Federal Reserve in employing economists. Amazon has opened stores where a customer can walk in, pick up what they want, and leave, with their credit cards automatically debited for the purchases made without needing to wait in a queue for checkout. This is a great innovation.

The banking system has undergone a phenomenal change. If banks do not innovate and adopt new systems, they will fail, as they will not be able to match the speed, conveniences, and security of the new banking system. In the next five years, I feel that 50% of the bank staff will not be required. We have an ATM to draw and deposit cash, and account information available online at the click of a button. With all this, there is very little need for a person behind the counter. In 2020, South Korea opened a full branch of a bank with no staff and it was completely computerized.

Innovation is a key area that is not clearly understood and implemented in India. Many people feel that small improvements in products or services is innovation. It is not. When there is continuous improvement, it can lead to path breaking developments, and that is innovation. As an example, solar panels produced today convert sunlight into electrical energy with an efficiency of about 17%. A Chinese company I know of can achieve an efficiency of 21% at the same cost. In a few years this company has the potential of being far ahead of similar companies. However, Panasonic has the patent for 25% efficient solar panels, and when this is commercially viable, it will revolutionise the solar power business because it will be cheaper than thermal power. This is real innovation.

CHAPTER FOURTEEN

Conclusion

In this book, I have presented actual case studies and learnings from great managers. Knowledge alone is not important. Using knowledge to convert ideas into reality and motivating people to perform to the best of their ability is the essence of management.

One has just to keep their mind open to see the array of opportunities that are spread before us at any point in time. We should be able to see these and pick up those relevant to us. Managers may be good or bad. It is for us to identify their good qualities and learn from them. We should question ourselves and ask what we have learnt every week or month and how we have implemented these at the workplace.

When companies recruit young managers, they try and assess their attitude and ability to learn. It does not matter if they do not have all the knowledge, provided they are willing to learn. I remember that in Tata International, the then HR head C.P. Joshi would always ask candidates about what they did to continue learning after they graduated from college.

In the stock market, we have people who can pick multi baggers. Companies too need to keep a tab on how many top-class managers they were able to recruit and retain, and how many they lost to competitors. In the early years, Tata Motors developed great talent by rigorous training, and though many left, they helped build the backbone of the auto industry in India. Companies like TCS, HUL, ITC, Tata Steel, NTPC have done a commendable job in training and retaining talent. Their succession planning has been meticulous, and they have not felt the need to recruit managers from other companies.

I would urge all young managers to read this book and build their own system for learning, improving and innovating at their place of work. This would make their job very interesting and help them to gain expertise and share their experience.

A job then, need not be one that just brings money. It will be something that one looks forward to every day and not just become a drudgery. Finally, what can beat the satisfaction of knowing that you have made the world just a bit better?

Printed in Great Britain
by Amazon